# Ethics in the Last Days of Humanity

# Ethics in the Last Days of Humanity

Don Cupitt

POLEBRIDGE PRESS
Salem, Oregon

Cover and interior design by Robaire Ream

**Library of Congress Cataloging-in-Publication Data**

Cupitt, Don, author.
  Ethics in the last days of humanity / by Don Cupitt.
      pages cm
  Includes bibliographical references and index.
  ISBN 978-1-59815-170-1 (alk. paper)
  1. Eschatology. 2. Humanity. 3. Twenty-first century--Forecasts. I. Title.
  BL500.C87 2016
  179'.1--dc23

                                                        2015031443

# Contents

# Introduction

## Predictions and Prophecies of Doom

Ever since the atomic bomb was used for the first—and so far the last—time as a weapon of war in 1945, human beings have had to live with the fear that one day we may be destroyed by our own technology. The doubts about our own long-term prospects as a species, and about what we are doing to our planet, have taken a great variety of forms. In many cases these fears have led to highly beneficial action in the sphere of public health, so that many city-dwellers now breathe much cleaner air and enjoy much purer water and better food than their grandparents had. People are also living much longer, so much longer that one can perhaps understand why "green" and climate change issues are not prominent in the British General Election campaigning that is going on as I write (in April 2015). People have heard it all before, but the worst predictions of doom have not been fulfilled, and life is still improving (even if somewhat slower than might be wished). People at large are still voting for growth.

Maybe in some areas we have recognized justice in the predictions of doom and have taken effective action to put things right. But other worries remain. There is the old Malthusian worry about how we can continue to feed a world population that is still increasing, from a land area that is being shrunk by overgrazing and desertification. There is the vast extinction of plant and animal species caused by, for example, the slow acidification of the sea by dissolved carbon dioxide, and the consequent melting away of coral reefs. And there is, perhaps most of all, climate change. This is an area in which there is widespread agreement among scientists, but it is also an area in which political resistance is very strong. There are many climate change deniers in individual countries (and some of them are in the pay of fossil-fuel interests), but we are also learning how little chance there is of persuading the largest carbon dioxide producers—the United States and China—to accept strict and legally-enforceable limits upon their own future emissions. The United Nations does not have, and is very unlikely ever to be given, the power to compel the largest polluters.

Now we begin to see some interesting ethical and religious questions arising. In astronomy and a few other areas we are accustomed to expect and to get very detailed and highly accurate predictions from the scientists. We would be astounded if an eclipse or a major storm were suddenly to appear quite unforeseen. So why do so many people doubt the seriousness of scientific warnings about global warming? The predictions follow in an ordinary way from well-established observations and laws of nature. In the developed countries, governments and courts of law are accustomed to taking expert scientific advice, and in Britain it seems that the major political parties are agreed that, whoever happens to be in power, the country will maintain its present policy of considerably increasing the percentage of our electricity that is produced by green and renewable means. So a certain amount of quiet adaptation is already going on in the hope that we will prove to have done enough to adapt ourselves to a leaner and greener future—along with other countries that are quietly doing much the same.

I suspect that the answer to the puzzle in all this is that the public and the deniers are suspicious about sermons from scientists. Scientific predictions are respected when they are deduced strictly rationally from well-established laws of nature and abundant detailed observations. Religious prophecies are very different: they usually threaten future divine punishment for grave moral lapses, and they are very rarely (if ever) successful. It is, people think, inappropriate that scientists, who should be grey and rational, should preach hellfire sermons about runaway global warming. By doing so they attract the well-deserved ridicule of climate change deniers.

I can now state the aims of this present essay.

First, just how seriously should we take the warnings about climate change? Is it probably, or almost certainly, true that we are already at or past the point of no return, so that very serious climate change is already unstoppable?

Secondly, what would be an appropriate religious response? It is very odd that religious groups have had so little to say, when novelists (for example) have written so many excellent and awesome stories about what may be coming to us all.[1]

And thirdly, what would be an appropriate ethic for us when we find ourselves living in the last days of the human race? When the hundreds of boatloads of refugees are struggling every day to cross the English Channel, should we be armed survivalists who shoot them; or should we welcome them and try with all our strength to incorporate them into our kibbutz-like groups that will be struggling to keep the old decencies alive?

And fourthly, if we are already entering our own eschaton, the last days of humanity, should we be urgently persuading people to give up as irrelevant all the older eschatologies of which vestiges still survive amongst us? Western Christianity, for example, has never officially abandoned its very elaborate traditional eschatology; but it is surely arguable that we should now forget all about the Second Coming, Christ's Millennial Reign on earth, the Last Trump, the Last Judgement, and heaven and hell. We need to drop all such ideas in order to clear our heads for the business of working out how we should be living during the last days of humanity. As I say, they have already begun. Or at least, they seem to have begun in those countries where the state has already broken down and life is dominated by fanatic militias. In such places children are growing up in ruined cities where the remains of the former population struggle for food and clean water, every day. Is this the future? Many young people in the West appear to think so, for they are running away from home in order to get to Syria and join the Islamic State. And their motives are described as idealistic.

They are actually *looking forward* to our ruined future!

# 1

# Self-Critical Religion Becomes Philosophy of Life

I first became strongly self-aware and reflective at the age of sixteen over sixty-five years ago. At once I found myself preoccupied with all the usual questions in the philosophy of life. What am I? What are *we*? What is our world, and in what way have we arisen within it, or become inserted into, or embedded within it? What can I know? How should I live? How can I set about attaining happiness, or the Good, or whatever I may come to think is the best I can hope for?

In modern times—and especially since about the 1660s—we have lived amidst a very rapid growth of scientific and historical knowledge. We have theorized and explained everything in sight. But the sense that my life is surrounded by utter mystery remains as strong as ever. It silences me, so that I find myself suspended in attentive contemplation of—of what? I guess you have probably very often had the same feeling. In the past, religious doctrine was so firmly entrenched in our culture and our thinking that it seemed to take the sting out of many or most of the great questions. Faith was confidence that we needn't worry too much about those matters, because God had them in hand. One could leave it to him. God had preordained the whole of your life, the date of your death, and the question of your final salvation. But with the decline of the old objective, world-controlling personal God, our sense of being securely destined has weakened drastically, leaving us thinking that our own selfhood and our life is in all its parts utterly contingent. Our life (like our entire life-world) is transient, fragile, and beautiful; a gauzy veil with nothing behind it.

There is a wonderful German word for this, which you must take pains to memorize: *unhintergehbarkeit*, "ungetbehindability". Our life and our experience is a streaming flux of contingent language-formed appearance—*with nothing behind it*. In my own vocabulary I devised and make much use of the term "outsidelessness", meaning thoroughgoing immanence. But I now rather wish I'd known about *unhintergehbarkeit* earlier. It's a better word than mine. The veil of sense is a façade—with no behind. As in late Claude Monet, there is no depth. There is only shimmering transience.

Wittgenstein, who was an anti-philosopher, says in effect that when we understand these ideas we see that nothing is hidden, and we are not missing anything. There is no mystery. There is no hidden metaphysical world beyond the veil of sense, and there is no esoteric knowledge possessed by an elite few. We can forget all such ideas, and then the problems of life will simply disappear. But I don't agree with him. On the contrary, I find, and I guess you may well agree, that after the end of metaphysics and of realistically understood religious belief, after the Death of God, we feel more than ever silenced, stumped, and confounded by the utter mysteriousness of our life.[2]

Put again, a little more clearly, *outsidelessness, unhintergehbarkeit,* immanence, means "nothing is guaranteed, nothing is objectively *founded*, nothing ever gets to be finally vindicated and assured. Instead we have only the delicate, lovely, interconnected web of ever shifting and flowing contingencies in which we are embedded, and which we call 'life'. Everything, everything just floats and fleets."

The mystery of life is back, then, and more absorbing than ever. After sixty-odd years of gazing at it and battling with it, I have made a little headway on some points here and there. Enough to have become able to say that I believe we can be happy if we learn to say yes to life, to live generously and without any ressentiment, to love the human life-world and humanitarian ethics, and to practise extravertive, solar living. Come out, present[3] and expend yourself. That's all, and it's all we need.

No doubt some of all that will be repeated in these pages. But in this book I have something new to discuss, as well. In the past thinkers would commonly tackle the big questions of popular philosophy by going back into the mythic past age when the world was first carved up, all the rules were laid down, and all the various kinds of living beings were installed in their proper places. The idea was that this story of how everything had first come to be the way it still is today, when told, will satisfy our doubts and questions. We'll shut up. As it was in the beginning, so it is now and ever shall be, world without end. For this kind of outlook, tradition, holy tradition, is deeply satisfying and consoling.

Unfortunately, such reassurances no longer work for us. Tradition seemed to promise us that the basic set-up of life was always as wise and good as it can be, from the beginning of the world until its end. It is all *fixed*, and does not need to be changed. It cannot be. But then in the early nineteenth century the new science of geology went historical, and suddenly persuaded us all that *not a single species* of living thing remains quite unchanging from the beginning of the world until its end. On the contrary, the fossil record makes it very clear that every species has only a finite period of life on earth. Once is has gone, it never, ever, comes back. And that includes us. We, the human species who have been clever enough to invent consciousness, knowledge, and values, we will one day be gone and forgotten forever. It will be as though we had never been.

So much was realized in the 1840s by the poet Alfred Tennyson (who by the general consent of other poets, led by Auden, was one of the stupidest men of his age), and then a generation later by the young Nietzsche (who was by far the brightest). Both were overwhelmed by the new realization of our human transience. We are destined not for eternity, but only for passing away into everlasting oblivion.

Another century on, the human situation has become more extreme still. Both runaway global warming and disastrous over-population may already be slipping beyond our control. We live with the awareness that a catastrophic collapse of our globalized, science-based industrial civilization is probably now unstoppable. We cannot even slow its acceleration into disaster. Many excellent dystopian novels have already been written by people like Russell Hoban, Doris Lessing and Cormac McCarthy with the aim of helping us to imagine what the ruined post-disaster world may be like for the few demoralized humans who survive in it, but in spite of their efforts religious thought has so far not made any contribution. This time it doesn't know how to flee from the wrath to come.

The aim of the present essay, then, is to open the question of religious and philosophical thinking at the end of history, at a time when the collapse of the world economy and of our civilization may be only two or three generations away. Seeing it all coming, the super-rich climate change deniers will by then have become survivalists who lay down stores and retreat to remote defensible locations in the mountains of the Far North, or into the security of the great cruise ships; but another century or so will quite probably see the end of them, and also of all the mobs of itinerant scavengers who have been seeking out and using up the remaining food and manufactured products. And children already born may live to see it happen. If that is our likely future, what do philosophers and people of religion now have to say about it?

The main thing to be said is that the prophesied disaster is itself *also a contingency*. It doesn't have to happen. It is possible that we are already beginning the changeover to renewable sources of electricity generation, that we are already rapidly improving battery technology and the insulation of buildings—in short, that we have already heeded the prophecy of doom sufficiently to be actively at work falsifying it. With a considerable effort, and some collective discipline, we may yet survive.

But the great Pentecostal shift towards a globalized humanitarianism, and away from mediated otherworldly religion towards a this-worldly mysticism of transient loveliness, will remain. The last age of mankind may last only a hundred years, or it may last indefinitely. Either way, I'm looking forward to it. And I mean that: *either* way. Reconciled to transience, we will not need the vanity of supposing that we will leave a long-term posterity of people who will remember us. Free from our old love of power, we will no longer feel the need for real and objective guarantees and commemorations. We will be happy to let go of all that.

# 2

# When a World Ends, the Old Morality Breaks Down

Following the pattern of ancient creation myths, most of the great philosophical systems set out to *establish* the world, rather than to threaten its impending collapse. The aim was usually to reassure the reader, and to stave off scepticism and dread. The world is rationally ordered and intelligible: it is our home, prepared for us by a benign Designer, and it has a built-in moral order. In the cosmic religion of European classical antiquity the world itself became an object of awed contemplation.[4] It was the unchanging and perfect night sky: it was heaven, or the heavens.

Kant has a little treatise on *The End of All Things*, but apart from that the topic of the end of the world was introduced into

Western philosophy by Hegel as a corollary to the discovery of time and historical development. In his optimistic historical vision Hegel pictures the whole of things as developing dialectically into a blessed and final totality. History was the autobiography of God: all of the world's and of our own plurality, relativity, contrariety, and imperfection is being taken up at last into God's own absolute unity, rationality, perfection, and joy in himself. Such is the End of All Things: it is a blessed consummation and already close enough to live by.

Hegel's optimism reflected the spirit of the German Enlightenment and the Romantic movement. All over Europe gifted younger people saw at first in the French Revolution a decisive and glorious historical advance. But the blissful new dawn did not last. The Revolution led soon to moral breakdown and the years of Terror. Eventually a new commercial and industrial society led by middle-class capitalists emerged, but it soon turned out to be falling a long way short of what people like Shelley and Godwin had hoped for. True, capitalism and steam-powered machinery quickly proved able to generate vast wealth, and there were some notable humanitarian reforms. But the labouring classes were little better off under their new masters, and the intellectual foundations of the new order were very weak and open to criticism. It was too often aggressively nationalistic and expansionist. From the 1830s one was constantly aware of a battle between optimistic and pessimistic interpretations of the way industrialism was developing. In the great manufacturing towns, slum housing, poor food, stinking rivers and epidemic disease made T. L. Peacock's Dr Opimian suggest that the "white slavery" in our English factories was little or no better than the "black slavery" in the American plantations, and that it might be "the destiny of science to destroy the human race".[5]

By this Peacock means more than that the new industries are already causing severe environmental pollution. He means also that the new cultural forces of science, technology, and capitalism are actively undermining traditional beliefs and values, and have in themselves no knowledge of any values other than their own nihilistic drive to ever-greater wealth and power. They were tending to make the whole of society into a machine that raced out of control towards its own self-destruction. Each new country that was colonized was seen as a stock of resources waiting to be exploited by swarming European hunters, loggers, and miners. Whole species, vast forests, and entire human peoples such as the Tasmanians were being simply wiped out. The nineteenth-century world was becoming gradually more humane in some respects—but in other respects it seemed crueller than ever.

During the first half of the century there was a considerable effort to keep pace with the rapid growth of population and the cultural changes that were going on in the big manufacturing cities of Britain and other Western countries. People strove to build enough churches and schools, and to create enough free-access public parks, museums, and galleries to maintain and even (as they hoped) to enhance the level of the inherited traditional culture. But by about 1850 it was becoming generally known that in the German universities critical philosophy and critical historical research had between them severely shaken the intellectual foundations of Western Christianity. In her youth during the 1840s the novelist George Eliot had translated important German writers such as Ludwig Feuerbach and David Friedrich Strauss into English, and a whole generation began to experience a crisis of faith. By the 1880s Nietzsche was writing, and as the modern movement in the arts and culture took shape, it took on an increasingly secular and even nihilistic character. Modernism in the arts did retain something of religious feeling amongst the followers of Van Gogh and amongst many of the abstract painters, but the loudest voices were very anti-Christian. They were followers of either Schopenhauer or Nietzsche. Human beings were going to have to grow a size larger. They could no longer live by passing on tradition. Instead, they must become creative.

They must make a fresh start, and create new values, new gods, a new world. The model human being was to be the great creative artist. Pessimists said, "If God is dead everything is permitted". Optimists replied, "If there is no God on earth, we must become gods ourselves".

The end of the old European culture was thus announced by a small group of intellectuals and artists in the last quarter of the nineteenth century. "Nihilism stands at the door".[6] The severity of the announcement could not be fully understood by most people for a few generations yet, during which Europeans' moral and cultural self-confidence was destroyed by a ruinous two-stage world war and the dissolution of the European colonial empires. During the twentieth century the explosively rapid growth of the world's population, of scientific knowledge, and of technology continued to race ahead. From 1945, when we were horrified by what the allied troops found when they entered the Nazi extermination camps, and then a few months later horrified again by what the first atomic bombs did to Hiroshima and Nagasaki, we have lived under the heavy shadow of severe pessimism about the long-term human prospect. Geologically, the epoch we now live in has come to be called the "Anthropocene", conventionally seen as beginning about the year 1610 in the Common Era. The geologists had opted for the year 1610 because it was the year in which Galileo first looked through a telescope at the moons of Jupiter. Since then the power and the rate of growth of our science and technology have steadily accelerated, until today our own human activities are the most obvious distinctive influence upon the whole world's geology. There have been about sixteen major scares during the seventy years since 1945, some threatening just the human future, and others threatening life on earth more generally. These scares have included a major thermonuclear exchange; a major natural disaster such as a big asteroid impact or the collapse of a large volcano into the ocean, in the Canaries or elsewhere, causing a "mega-tsunami", a vast racing shock-wave of water; extreme environmental pollution by insecticides, nitrates, and fluorocarbons or other chemicals; progressive desertification, leaving insufficient land for food production; loss of male fertility in consequence of environmental pollution; overpopulation; mineral resource exhaustion; runaway global warming caused chiefly by the release of too much carbon dioxide into the atmosphere, and then exacerbated by the additional large-scale release of methane from the tundra—and so on. Some combination of these factors still seems likely to lead, during the next century or so, to a major extinction event, such as has occurred on a few occasions in the past.

Next we note that the political organization of humankind into well over two hundred nation states, each a rational egoist committed to living by a narrative of its own hard-won independence and steadily increasing wealth and power, makes it quite likely impossible for us to make an organized and enforced transition to world economic sustainability. Every international gathering becomes a chorus of voices demanding money from the West in general, and from the Americans in particular. The cries vary a little. "The Americans are chiefly to blame and the Americans must pay"; "We're doing nothing until the Americans have done everything"; "We will play *our* part *after* we have caught up with the Americans, and not until then". Since the Americans collectively, since the 1940s, have been by a significant margin the world's largest, most powerful, most successful, and in many ways also the most generous country, I need not trouble the reader by pointing out just how unimpressed they are by all this shallow anti-Americanism, which in recent years has tended to develop into anti-intellectual suspicion of all things Western. It remains just possible that a technical fix for global warming will be discovered in time, and if so we can be pretty sure that it will be the Americans who discover it and then rush to install it. It might involve large-scale decarbonisation of the atmosphere, coupled with the production of energy and food by some managed version of photosynthesis, or perhaps nuclear fusion. It is also just possible that we are already making piecemeal adjustments, so that our consumption becomes gradually more efficient and thrifty, and so will ward off the worst threats that face us. But the hour is already very late, and the most likely future for us all is that most human beings will remain so addicted to their old tribal and national loyalties, and to their old demands for growth, that they will not be persuaded unanimously to accept many decades of severe economic austerity. Instead, we may expect to see more and more failed nation-states, more and more economic collapse leading to vast tides of economic migrants seeking a country, *any* country, where they can find work and food. The scale of the suffering ahead is barely imaginable.

All this is only too familiar. Much less familiar but even more important is the scale and the horror of the *moral* breakdown which will accompany those events. It has already begun. We have for some years now been witnesses of what has already happened on a large scale in some parts of Africa, the Middle East, and India.

Some of these horrors are traditional. They have only recently been generally exposed to our appalled gaze, but historians will say that they are not new. The sex-murder and gross mutilation of women, the severe abuse of babies, FGM (female genital mutilation), the smiling decapitation on camera of helpless prisoners, child soldiers, the torture of detainees, and drawn-out public executions—often in the past people simply preferred not to leave us much documentary evidence and description of such things. One did not dwell upon such horrors. Much of our literature was meant to be edifying, and to leave our innocence uncorrupted.

Nevertheless, we cannot be unaware that our modern moral breakdown has already become exceptionally severe and widespread even by historical standards. Morality is always culturally embedded. People derive the moral standards that constrain them from the cultural totality or world within which they live. It may be a *tribe*, it may be the *city-state*, it may be one of the great *religions*, it may be a *nation-state*, or it may be one of our modern large and now very *multi-faith and multi-ethnic states.* To live peacefully as a member of one of these five different types of society, you need to internalize and become habituated to its internally-evolved morality and its way of life; but during the twentieth century hundreds of millions of people found themselves making a very abrupt transition from one of them to another, further along the line. They have found it acutely disorienting. It feels like a complete moral breakdown, the end of a familiar world. Reconstruction is not easy. Unfortunately, when the great colonial empires were dissolved in the mid-twentieth century, people—in Africa, for example—were given little or no advice on how to make the moral transition from being a tribesman to being a citizen of a modern democratic nation-state. It is a huge change: many people completely lose their bearings, or their moral compass.

Today, this situation is worsening fast. As recently as the 1950s to 1970s, we assumed that the nonviolent way was morally preferable in the struggle for nuclear disarmament, or for black civil rights in the United States. But today the shockingly ruthless violence of ISIS (The Islamic State in Syria) and of Boko Haram in Nigeria seems to have a positive moral *attraction* for young people in Europe. People are drawn to extreme violence and martyrdom, as if they suspect that it is the future for all of us.

I am suggesting, then, that we live in an era of very rapid advance in science and technology, and of economic globalization. Billions of people have already found that they are being "detraditionalized". Their ancient cultures and faiths are dying on them. They find themselves morally and religiously denuded and disoriented. Some of them may think it possible to violently reinstate traditional religious identity. They are the *fundamentalists*. Others try to reinstate absolute *social* authority. They vote readily for strong leaders. Others join militias and fight, endlessly, just for themselves. Young men who have become accustomed to living by their guns find it very difficult to give them up.

Are there any better options? In Western culture generally, and in all parts of the world influenced by it, by far the best thing we have left to cling to as we face a very dark future is our tradition of *humanitarian ethics* originally associated in the Bible with the last and blessed Age to Come at the end of time, and now diffused very widely through the *Universal Declaration of Human Rights*; through the United Nations and its various agencies concerned with refugees, health, food and the like; through the modern state's active concern to promote the education, the health and the welfare of its subjects; and through the great international voluntary aid organizations. Consider, for example, the heroic and largely voluntary efforts of the medical workers who have recently risked, and in many cases given, their lives to get the West African Ebola outbreak under control. This great and remarkable ethical tradition nowadays influences a wide range of professional codes. It is built into the way the British National Health Service (NHS) functions, so strongly that although one-third of all employees are immigrants from a very wide range of faiths and backgrounds, they somehow absorb and learn to practise the ethic with aplomb. Voters who often voice anti-immigrant views, when they become NHS in-patients, seem not to notice that they are receiving dedicated service and often very great calmness and forbearance from the very immigrants whom they in other contexts dislike and regard as aliens.

The many considerations just sketched have been intended to introduce a thesis that will seem to most people at first very surprising. It is that *humanitarianism is eschatological*, and it is a very important insight.

Very briefly, the leading figures of the political Enlightenment, culminating in people like Godwin and Shelley and others, were utopian optimists. They believed that the progressive growth of knowledge and the liberation of people's minds from traditional superstition would gradually bring about the comprehensive liberation of humanity. "The perfectibility of man" was the great slogan, and in the French Revolution for a while even the most highly gifted people of all (for example, Beethoven, Wordsworth, and even Kant himself) watched events in France with great excitement. Their hopes were being realized.

They were disappointed as they saw what followed—moral breakdown, the Terror, middle-class nationalism, capitalism at its most extreme and vandalistic, and fears that accelerating population growth would soon far outrun the land's capacity to feed the people. By the mid-nineteenth century it was noted in England that most of the people now lived in the cities. The country was becoming dependent upon imported food. In short, imperial expansion was necessary in order to secure markets for our industrial products and the supply of food for the home population. But underlying all these familiar themes is the greater one of the continuing enormous growth of scientific knowledge and of new technologies. It has steadily secularized and "detraditionalized" us all—and when the imperial powers of Europe came into conflict with each other, it made the great two-stage war between them (of 1914–18, and then of 1938–45) all the more destructive.

Now, in the early twentieth century many of the leaders of society were still classically educated. When they heard the Great War of 1914–18 described as "the war to end wars" they could not fail to remember themes from classical thought. Since the late Bronze Age early speculative thinkers had been horrified by the periods of warring states—long periods when bloody war seemed to be the normal relationship between states. All young men were raised to be warriors. In almost all early civilizations martial ardour was greatly admired, and peoples endlessly, bloodily, and uselessly battled to destroy each other. Why is man a wolf to man, *homo homini lupus*? The great moral teachers of the Axial period, and some of the religious mythmakers too, dreamt of a Last Battle and of the coming of a globalized, multi-ethnic world in which people have finally freed themselves from tribalism and nationalism, and have learnt to live at peace with each other. It would be the Last Age of humanity, the Kingdom of God on Earth.

Modern humanitarian ethics has many distinguished sources. In Britain we think of the long line of great Victorian social re-formers, and more recently of the heroes of the post-war Labour government of Clement Attlee. In the Americas one thinks of the long, hard struggle, still going on, for the full social emanci-pation of the many non-white indigenous and imported peoples. Gradually, also, concern for the welfare of the victims of war and the poorest in one's own society has extended across the entire world. One thinks especially of the International Committee of the Red Cross, of the Geneva Conventions, and of liberal social-democratic Scandinavia; but it is worth noting that most con-servatives were inclined to ridicule and to oppose the advance of humanitarianism until the word suddenly conquered, and came into everyday use in about 1990. The medical profession fought hard against the establishment of the NHS in 1947: today mem-bers of it are often themselves distinguished humanitarians. The employers (or "masters" as they used to be called) during the pe-riod of the Industrial Revolution fought against workers' rights and any kind of minimum wage all the way: but happily most of them are now converted.

Today, we are almost all of us humanitarians—because we darkly suspect that the human race has not got much time left. The way the human situation has developed since 1800 has meant that we can no longer refer the authority of the ethical to anything "out there"—in the supernatural world, or in the way Nature goes, or in one's own people's tradition of social author-ity. Our situation is eschatological in the sense that we can no longer ground ethics in the law of God, or nature, or society.

All that is passing away; it's dying on us, because inevitably the death of God is followed by the death of creation and the death of man. Our received historical world has come to its end. Because nobody out there loves us, we must love one another. Humanitarianism is the ethic for the end of time, the ethic of an age when we have finally come to see that we are on our own. We must remake good and evil for ourselves. This is the ethic of the early, and especially of St Luke's, Jesus, and now it has become all we have, the most precious bit remaining to us of what we have inherited from the past.

So "humanitarianism", the word, arrived and established itself as the best ethic we have left to us at just the moment—perhaps at the height of the flower-power popular utopianism of the 1960s—when we began to understand that a change of dispensation is under way. We felt that we must begin to choose the values and outlook of the "Kingdom of God on earth". Instead of being very long-termist in our outlook, as in the past, people at the pop festivals were looking for paradise now, eternal happiness in the present moment.

This was instant religion, at a time when people began to feel that humanity's days on earth are now coming to an end. The times are nihilistic: Some young Muslims may love, admire, and want to join the Islamic State's popular executioner, who coolly cuts off innocent people's heads on camera. That is Islamic anti-humanism and it is the purest theism. But if you are a post-Christian humanitarian, you admire Mr William Pooley, who persists in venturing his life in trying to stem an outbreak of Ebola in West Africa. That is Christian humanism and many Muslims are implacably opposed to it. Soon, both groups of people will be gone for ever. For ever. But you need to ask yourself whom you wish to go with.

# 3

# Eschatological Humanism

## The Revelation of Man at the End of History

The historical life of human beings is life under discipline—domestic, scholastic, religious, and above all military. Order, security must be maintained. People are organized into tribes, ethnic groups or nations, and social leadership is principally and primarily military. Even today, in easy-going democratic Britain, the Queen is still, as head of state, head of the armed forces, and every young prince in the direct line of succession to the throne serves for short periods with the Royal Army, the Royal Navy, and the Royal Air Force. At the top of society, the profession of arms is still the noblest profession, and war remains part of life. As I write, another young soldier has been awarded the Victoria Cross for risking his life to save a comrade. But as we have pointed out earlier, aid workers with Médecins Sans Frontières /Doctors without Borders or the World Health Organization (WHO) who take similar risks do not receive the same honours. Mere medics are simply not as important as soldiers. Killing is nobler than healing.

There is a striking example of our continuing addiction to military values in the young Wordsworth. He has a sonnet in which he complains that England has become corrupt and decadent, because men have "changed swords for ledgers". Despite his youthful idealism, Wordsworth still thinks that the businessmen and the bankers who create and maintain prosperity are ignoble human beings, or at least, are so in comparison with soldiers.

The First World War was so spectacularly murderous and futile that it prompted many novel protests which became famous. "Patriotism is not enough", "I must have no hatred in my heart towards anyone", "I am the enemy you killed, my friend". Almost for the first time, people were willing to die as conscientious objectors to military service. For almost the very first time people were prompted by their hazy memories of the Bible to contemplate the coming of a new age in which competitive nationalism and the military ethic would lose their ancient authority and become obsolete.

The biblical echoes in our modern humanitarianism are very strong. There are a number of striking examples of human compassion towards the poor in the Torah, and the prophets are agreed that the first characteristic of the new and better world they long to see is that it will be a world of international peace, a world in which "nation speaks peace unto nation", and there is no more war. In the Gospel, Jesus' own performance of humanitarian actions is a sign that the New Age has begun, or is coming in, and he speaks openly and freely with a variety of non-Jews. He is not ethnocentric: he is an internationalist. But the most vivid example in the New Testament is the treatment of the Day of Pentecost in the Acts of the Apostles. Representatives of the major nations are present, and the divine spirit is poured out upon them all. The new age of "eschatological human-ism" begins. We are assured that the early Christians practised community of goods. Minor officers called deacons (in Greek, "ministers") collected money for the relief of poor saints in other lands, and for other good causes.

This celebrated biblical precedent was followed by those who first set up and worked for the League of Nations and the United Nations. It was hoped that these organizations would turn out to be the forerunners of some kind of world government. They also opened an era of official world humanitarian concern, in which through their various agencies relief would be channelled to refugees, to the victims of plague, to the poor and the hungry, and so on.

The initial hopes for the UN may not have been realised in full, but at least there has not been another world war. Perhaps we do understand somehow that there *cannot* be another world war. And interestingly, the new technologies that could destroy us also make us highly sensitive to human need all round the world. As I write, the Vanuatu archipelago in the Pacific Ocean on the far side of the globe, has been hit by a very severe cy-clone. The whole world instantly heard all about it, and huge aircraft laden with blankets, fresh water bottles, food, and medi-cal supplies were landing within two days of the disaster. In the historical period you felt human sympathy for troubled people who were close to you, but today's Pentecostal humanitarian-ism is new. It is also the norm, now: everyone expects it. Since about 1980 or 1990 we seem to have become aware that we may now be living in the last days of mankind, and our sympathies have widened accordingly. The great shadow hanging over us all has the effect of making us huddle together. Just compare our response to Vanuatu with mainland Britain's response in the early nineteenth century to the Irish potato famine. John Stuart Mill was already teaching a form of universal humanist ethics, but it was to be at least another century before the bulk of us began to *feel* the same way. One smiles when one sees that the victims of a major natural disaster—an earthquake or a great storm—feel entitled to *expect* help to come speedily from overseas. If they live in a remote mountainous area they are likely to greet the Western aid workers who bring them their supplies with the cry: "Why did it take you so long?" Quite right: they *demand* our total generosity, because that is increasingly the ethic we profess to live by. Think, in Britain, of the National Blood Transfusion Service, or of those who donate organs for transplant. We want, and we rightly expect, people to be extremely generous by historical standards.

It is comical that people should nowadays expect and even *demand* of the West an ethic of total generosity, but I am glad of it. And from where do we get this ethic of supernatural, and almost impossible, generosity? From Jesus, of course. Not from the Christ of developed ecclesiastical Christianity, which got Jesus very badly wrong, but from the Jesus of history, the moral teacher, the eschatological humanitarian. Goodish traditions of Jesus' teaching were preserved by some of his followers until the late 40s, about fifteen years after his death. But then, with the rise of supernatural Christological doctrine, the moral teaching of Jesus was increasingly revised, and even reversed in meaning, by his own professed followers. Enough survived, happily, for me to be able to point by name to the early Jesus, as the teacher of the "words of the Lord" as they were heard and remembered from about 30 to 48.

A simple way of learning to recognize the early Jesus begins by looking up the traditional Sermon on the Mount, and learning to look out for the glaring contradictions in Jesus' reported teaching. Very soon two very distinct teachers will appear. They hold sharply contrasting views.

1. Was Jesus (a) a short-termist, who commended immediate, impulsive action? Or was he (b) a long-termist, who advised prudent calculation before you commit yourself?

2. Did Jesus advocate (a) an ethic of "solar self-outing" which has us putting on a brave show in public; or did he teach (b) a spirituality of hidden inwardness, which requires us to conceal our true religious life, inwardly and secretly referring everything to eternity, in the hope of an eternal reward hereafter?

3. Does Jesus believe (a) in only *one* world, the Kingdom of God established on this earth; or (b) does he believe and live in *two* worlds, this life which is a period of probation, and the afterlife, in which the faithful will be rewarded?

4. Is Jesus (a) highly critical of the traditional ethic of obedience to religious law, on the grounds that a law ethic can never produce the kind of whole-hearted spontaneous love, even for your enemy, that he seeks; or (b) did Jesus in effect reconfirm the mosaic law, even to the extent of internalizing it and tightening it up?

5. Was Jesus (a) an ethical activist who thinks we must learn to live by our own feelings, and in particular by love alone? Or was he (b) a moral realist who thinks that moral judgments are made true or false by things and qualities out there, such as written lawcodes and the objective purity or impurity of things?

6. Did Jesus argue that (a) every one of us must learn to be quite spontaneously loving and unconditionally generous, having the courage to make the first move towards reconciliation; or did he (b) argue that because *God* has generously taken the initiative and forgiven us our sins, we ought *in response* readily to forgive others ourselves?

I'll stop there because that is enough to make the main point. The early Jesus can still be traced in the Sermon on the Mount (Matthew 5, 6), expressly teaching all the (a)s above. But—presumably as the influence of men like Paul grew—Jesus' teaching was severely censored and revised to construct a new, more Catholic and monkish Jesus. Pretty much, you may observe, as Vatican officials today hasten to reinterpret Pope Francis when he makes the mistake of talking too spontaneously and sounding too like the early Jesus.

It is easy to learn to tell the early Jesus from the Catholic Jesus as you read the Synoptic Gospels. But you may well wonder why in the entire history of Christian thought nobody seems to have noticed and thought about the obvious conflict within the teachings of Jesus that have been transmitted to us. Not even quite intelligent people like Kierkegaard and Tolstoy, both of whom are usually regarded as major geniuses, saw the problem. The only answer I can give is that as soon as the major Christological beliefs had become attached to Jesus, he was treated as an oracle. His words were divine commands, "the Law of Christ". It was no longer possible to think critically about what you were hearing. So the Church did its best to wipe out and forget the original Jesus, in the way illustrated by Dostoyevsky in *The Brothers Karamazov*.[7] Hence the good-humoured self-description of the Fellows of the Jesus Seminar of themselves as attempting the seemingly impossible task of "smuggling Jesus into Christianity". The difference today is that since the work of Albert Schweitzer and Rudolf Bultmann in the early twentieth century it has become easier to make and to see a clear distinction between the (pre-Christian) message of Jesus, who was a man and an original thinker and teacher; and the (Christian) message *about* him. All I have done is to press that point harder, and to say that the early Jesus is a much greater figure than the divine Christ.

Note that for the early Jesus, the end of history and the coming of the Kingdom of God is the age when "the Son of Man" is revealed. The disciplinary period comes to an end, and the morally-adult human being stands forth. Such human beings are no longer under law: they are autonomous, a law unto themselves. Jesus appears as an ethical Prometheus who steals from heaven and has given to us the power to rule upon questions of right and wrong.[8] "Why do you not judge for yourselves what is right?" (Luke 12:57). At the end of history all the old ruling authorities are revealed to have been paper tigers. They pass away, and we understand that *we* must become the creators of good and evil, as we are also the sole creators of our world. Jesus is the moral liberator who saves us, not from our sins, but from the very concept of sin. He saves us from the government of our life by religious law. He delivers us, in particular, from ideas of ritual purity and impurity. Instead we must now learn to live by our own open hearts, without any ressentiment or ill feeling at all towards anyone. In later centuries, Kantians, Marxists, and Nietzscheans took up and tried to elaborate this theme of the coming at last of a new and fully adult human being, but Jesus' own version of the doctrine remains much the best. Strange that (with the possible exception of the heretic Marcion) no Christian ever observed that Jesus was a spectacularly good moral *thinker*.

Interestingly, the Way, the faith we eventually came to call Christianity, as it developed came to see itself as living in a dual world. Two different orders coexist, in society and within the individual life. On the large scale, the old historical world of universal reciprocal prickliness, military preparedness, chronic rivalry, and incipient conflict still continues. But there are everywhere at least *a few* seeds and green shoots of Jesus' new world. They can be found in various private enclosed little worlds such as those of the family, the religious house, the congregation, various charitable enterprises, and so on. But it was usually taught that "the persistence of concupiscence in the baptised" means that we cannot expect everybody to be able to live in public by Jesus' top standard, the *consilia* or "counsels of perfection". Not yet. The world is not ready for it, and the Luther-to-Reinhold-Neibuhr tradition says that the compelling but impossible ethic of Jesus presently functions to remind us of our own imperfection and our need of divine grace. Luther's religion ended by being rather gloomy. The believer struggles on, but never sees in this life the longed for victory. The streets remain mean. From Marlowe to Wallander, the modern detective has been a Lutheran.

Such was the orthodox settlement, for centuries. But I have suggested that events in the twentieth century overthrew it. People in the Tolstoy and Gandhi tradition wanted to live the ethics of the Sermon on the Mount and to prove that it is entirely practicable in this life. For example, pacifists and conscientious objectors to war were ready to accept severe punishment for the stand they took. In the early twentieth century those who battled to establish universal suffrage and the League of Nations were trying to entrench bits of Jesus' Kingdom-ethic, his humanitarianism, within the present still-historical order. It has been done with such success that even within the poorest and most backward third-world countries, the average expectation of life was more than doubled during the twentieth century—from around 28 to around 60 years. The same period has been very destructive, and we have seen many morally horrific things happen. We have also found many reasons for fearing that the human race is rapidly heading for technological self-destruction. Furthermore, even as we can report a few successes for non-violent political struggle, population growth goes roaring ahead, and seems likely to cancel out any successes we may have in other areas.

But now the central irony: we begin to see a number of seemingly-disparate themes—moral breakdown as the old order decays, humanity's self-destruction by its own roaring technological development, the steady advance of globalized humanitarian ethics, and the gradual emergence of a single world moral consciousness strongly influenced not by Christianity but by

Jesus—these disparate themes are all becoming interwoven in the complex story that I am trying to tell.

We seem to be living through the Last Things. In parts of Africa and the Middle East the moral decay of the older order is giving rise to almost incomprehensible horrors: it's as if we are living through the birthpangs of a new humanity, now taking shape. The Tribulations, or the Messianic Woes. Or perhaps we are simply heading into the simple cessation of all life on Earth by runaway climate change during the next century or so?

# Appendix

Look at the *Oxford English Dictionary* for the early history of the word "humanitarian". Originally a theological term for a christological doctrine that laid almost all the emphasis upon Jesus' humanity rather than his divinity, it was switched to mean something more like "philanthropic" in the 1830s and 1840s. In Britain, F. W. Robertson of Brighton was a key figure, but conservative thinkers long tended to ridicule humanitarians for being soft and wet. Only since the BandAid concert of 1984 in support of Ethiopia has *humanitarian* come into everyday use with strongly favourable overtones. Even as late as 1998, *The New Oxford Dictionary of English* still does not like the word.

My shocking argument is that our everyday use of the word humanitarian, and our general acceptance of humanitarian ethics, proves that we know ourselves to be already living in the last days of humanity. My main supporting argument is that since the end of metaphysics (or roughly, since Ludwig Feuerbach) all forms of moral realism have died. Everything out there in which we might have hoped to ground morality—God, religion, tradition, nature, society—has melted away. We stand utterly alone, with nothing left to live by except what comes out of our own hearts, that is, our feeling for each other. Jesus was the first teacher of this ultra-radical doctrine, but there have been others since Blake and Nietzsche. Hence my view that although the church-religion of Christianity is now dead, Jesus has quite recently become bigger than ever. Only human and post-theistic, he is the Son of Man, now manifest as a cosmic figure.

I should add a few words in explanation of my use of phrases such as "solar ethics" and "solar living". As is said above, I see the early Jesus as the teacher of an ethic of immediate and gener-ous self-outing. One should not live a hidden religious life, try-ing to preserve the self for the eternal world. The self should be spent, not saved. As Jesus puts it: "Let your light so shine before men that they may see your good works...."

# 4

# The Second Adam

I have been drawing an analogy between, on the one hand, the very remarkable ethical teaching of Jesus, seen in the context of the strained and fantastical mood of his times, and our ethical situation in our own day, when our science and technology have developed so much and so rapidly that they have surrounded us almost completely. Culture has long been described as a protective screen, a second nature, within which we shelter ourselves from wild, inhospitable nature. Today this protective screen of culture—which includes language, general world-view, scientific knowledge, technology, material culture, and so forth—has become so big that our best and most popular science fiction writing and cinema is now about almost nothing *but* technology. We live inside what has now become an entirely man-made reality. Its violence, and the difficulty of preventing it from running out of control and destroying us, gives us our feeling of being threatened by our own products.[9] They are more up to date than we are. We feel we are becoming redundant. We live with the knowledge that we have made ourselves vulnerable and now must struggle to maintain and to reaffirm our confidence in our own life, and our ordinary human-animal feelings.

Drawing an analogy between the cultural situation in Jesus' time and that of today—as seen, perhaps, in films like *Blade Runner* and *I, Robot*—may help us to see why then and now ethics took the form of a struggle to find ways of saying yes to life, affirming human values, and living ardently, extravertively, and without anxiety in the present moment. We need to oppose the domination of our life by instrumental values (preferring always the most rational, efficient engineering solutions to all problems) and by our seemingly insatiable desire for yet more growth in consumption and in power. Instead, we should switch our attention to art, to display, and to the emotions. We need to defeat the bad old habit that always draws disparaging contrasts between reason and the passions. On the contrary, it is feeling alone that makes us human. Without it, we are as dead as our machines.

For various reasons people, both in biblical times and nowadays, have felt themselves to be living in the last times. Everything is passing away: the human race may feel threatened by extinction, or near-extinction, within a century from today. I am in my 80s, and thinking about what my grandchildren may soon have to cope with. How shall we all live with what is surely coming? I have answered in terms of "solar ethics" for today—an ethical doctrine established purely philosophically and without any appeal to authority or to religious law—and I have argued that in recent scholarship the original Jesus of Nazareth is seen as having taught something very similar. One should live as the sun does, by generous self-outing.

Then and now, when everything is passing away, human beings are deprived of all the external things that used to give them moral guidance: religious authority, social authority, tradition, and nature. All these things are crumbling fast. Nor can we pin our hopes upon a better long-term future. That's gone too. There is unlikely to be any better future. What do we have left to us? Only each other. Ethics, for Jesus and for us, has to become thoroughly and consistently humanitarian. While life remains—and we do not know how long that may be—we need an ethic of public self-outing and display—"shining", Jesus calls it, his habitual metaphors being highly visual—that keeps human feeling and human values firmly impressed upon all that we deal with and do. We must resolutely resist dehumanization, or the devaluation of life.

At this point you may interpolate an objection. Solar living is not and cannot be our *only* response to the threatened end of humanity. There is also the Jonah paradox. The prophet Jonah, you will remember, was sent by God to warn the people of Babylon that unless they repented their misdeeds they were doomed. As it turned out, the people of Babylon heard the prophecy, repented—and were spared. Similarly today, we who have heard the scientific warnings about climate change find ourselves fighting on various fronts. We tell the climate change deniers that the warnings really are serious, and at the same time many of us are already responding to the threat by installing renewable electricity generation, insulating our houses and so on. If we do all this at once sufficiently energetically, we may succeed in averting, or at least deferring for a while, the threat of runaway climate change, by continuously adjusting our own behaviour in response to its approach. But when that happens, we'll surely appear to have falsified our own initial prophecy, and to have given the advantage to the climate change deniers. They will crow over us—but then they will learn that by the strenuousness of their own denial that climate change is coming, they have made it inevitable, because they have persuaded us not to do enough to stop it. Thus the Jonah paradox works both ways.

The central paradox here—that a prophetic warning which *succeeds* in changing people's behaviour thereby *fails* as a prediction of doom—cannot be avoided. In reply, I acknowledge that we should of course attempt to do what we can to cut our consumption of fossil fuels, and we should try to persuade the sceptics. But I still put solar living first. In times when we are beset by huge, daunting doubts and uncertainties, it is still the best policy, whatever happens. Our human be-ing is always utterly contingent, and unsupported by anything out there. Solar living is always the best and only comfort; and especially so when people are tempted to despair. Live in the moment, live by your heart.

This relentless determination, however tough things may get to be, and however much we are opposed by some of our own fellow humans, to affirm the values of life in general and of our own human feeling-life in particular, is purely this-worldly. There is no supernatural order, and there are no supernatural beings or powers. There is simply no evidence for them. At the end of all things everything is seen to be utterly fragile, baseless, and transient. The old platonic contrast between the world of eternal forms and the world of transient fact can no longer be drawn. We can no longer look for help and guidance to anything beyond the here and now. Our affirmation of life and of human feeling has to be 100 percent, and entirely presentist. Solarity is, amongst other things, total absorption in our living, our work and our relationships.

All these things are said with admirable and exemplary clarity by the early Jesus. He seems to have begun by radicalizing the teaching of the major Israelite prophets, who had all taught that Israel's received religion of sacred law had not succeeded. The code of divine law, promulgated, read out in public, interpreted,

and applied to human life, in all sorts of ways had failed to produce the righteous individuals and the good society that Israel
and Israel's God wanted to see. The prophets hoped to see the
written law replaced by a new immediate religion of the heart.
People's lives would be made good not by their conformity to
external rules about purity, impurity and the like, but by being
inspired by generous and wholehearted human feeling. Jesus
makes the very anthropocentric point of this in various ways:
by saying that human need is more important in prompting immediate moral action than is religious law; by insisting that the
Sabbath was made for man, and not man for the Sabbath; and
by saying that people's conduct is made pure or impure by what
comes *out of* them and not by what goes *into* them (Mark 7:15,
and note the interpretations of this offered by Matthew 15:10–
20; and Luke 11:37–40). Most Christian readers do not grasp
just how "anthropomonist" all this is, and they do not grasp
how radical is the brief observation: "Why do you not judge for
yourselves what is right?" But by saying this Jesus really is shifting the power of determining good and evil—or, as ordinary
language puts it, deciding "the difference between right and
wrong"—from God to us. The old lawgiver God dies, and is replaced by the first morally-adult and autonomous human beings.
They keep God as a guiding spiritual ideal: love is God (1 John
4:7–21). But the human being is from now on the undisputed
centre and arbiter of the human moral world—a doctrine that
can be maintained consistently only if our self-understanding
becomes radically egalitarian and democratic. In the old humanity, all human relations (except possibly the relation to one's
twin) were unequal. You were always acutely aware of whether
the person before you was your social superior or inferior. There
was always an order of seniority. But in the new humanity all are
equal and they *must* be so.[10]

Now we see why the most interesting and lastingly important
of the New Testament titles of Jesus is the one that refers to

him as the Second Adam, or the Last Man (see especially Paul's Epistle to the Romans, chapter 5). It is a non-supernaturalist title, but a grand one nevertheless, for it affirms that in Jesus all humanity, the entire concrete universal *Humanum*, makes a fresh start. He is the pioneer, the first of many. Nietzsche missed this: he thought humanity became fully adult, or at least potentially so, in the cheek of wily characters like Odysseus and Abraham, the first men who had the nerve to argue back against their gods. But Nietzsche admitted that after Abraham and Odysseus there had been a relapse as the great lawgivers (Solon, Moses, and so on) restored the government of humans by patriarchy and disciplinary institutions. But I don't think even Nietzsche quite understood the nature of Jesus' radicalism. Perhaps Marcion, usually remembered as the first great post-apostolic theologian and the first important heretic, remains the individual who has come closest to understanding Jesus. As he sees it, Jesus' gospel of pure love is bound to put an end to the religion of law, because pure, spontaneous and undeserved love cannot ever be commanded by law. Therefore the early Jesus is the Death of the old God, as I see it.

If and when Jesus—the early Jesus—is successfully disentangled from the received main tradition of his teaching, and is heard and understood, he will very likely come to be recognized as the brilliant pioneer of the *religious* Enlightenment, and the first teacher to take a fully adult and critical view of *homo religiosus*, man the religious being. He was the first to teach "empty solar humanism" as the last religious philosophy of life, and the one that I personally plan to go out on. I know of no credible alternative to it, except perhaps the yellow-hat version of Tibetan Buddhism.

Interestingly, a surprising amount of orthodox Christian doctrine about Christ returns to us in the radical humanist interpretation of his teaching that I propose. He was such a blasphemer by the standards of the old religious outlook, that he must be condemned to die by the old outlook in order to liberate us from it. His generic humanity returns in the way in which he incorporates us into himself as we begin to live in the novel way that he first taught. And so on. Christians may wish to recuperate much of the old doctrine about Christ along these lines. My own feeling is that we can no longer base our lives upon disputable critical reconstructions of ideas, teachings, people, and so on from the remote past. So I have been careful to put forward a purely-philosophical defence of solar ethics. I do not make it dependent upon Jesus. Personally, I would stick with it even if it were to turn out that Jesus never lived. But in fact it seems to me that he taught it, and for that I still revere him.

# 5

# Eschatologies, Ancient and Modern

In different periods the task of articulating society's basic world picture has been allocated to different groups, using often very different vocabularies. In Bronze-Age times people recited their creation stories in the language of religious myth, as in Genesis. Later, the Greek philosophers Plato, Aristotle, and Claudius Ptolemy held sway for two millennia, until they were finally displaced by the mathematical physics of Isaac Newton. More recently, since Einstein, things have been changing again—very rapidly.

However, some things remain the same. In all ages there is respect and admiration for nature as an orderly, beautiful and harmonious system. But if we ask: "What *keeps* everything in its place and following its proper rhythm?" we are given rather different answers at different times. Earlier, we might have been told that everything just *likes* to keep in the place and to follow the rhythm that the gods have appointed for it. Later, the order of things is seen as the product of a self-maintaining, self-correcting balance of conflicting forces. Later again, nature becomes a kind of ecosystem: whether we are talking of living organisms or of electrically charged particles, things tend to jostle each other and settle down into a richly-woven interdependent texture.

At all times, however, we are likely to meet the idea that too great a disturbance of nature's balance will lead to disaster. Hence the at first-surprising formal similarity between eschatologies ancient and modern. Today's climate change and related environmental debates are not led either by people of religion, nor even by philosophers, at all. They are led by professional scientists, together with a few allies and supporters in the media and politics. But, surprisingly, their language is traditional: "If we carry on like this, we'll be heading for a major disaster. We must repent, and change our lives before it's too late."

This formal resemblance between eschatologies modern and ancient calls for discussion. When we hear leading scientific figures, such as for example the astronomer royal Lord Rees (or Sir Martin Rees), talking the language of prophets of doom, we are puzzled. Many politicians are puzzled. As Tony Blair and some others have put it, the issue is so big, so overarching, and so general that it is hard to know just what one is expected to do about it right now. It is too big to handle at the same time as one is coping with the small matters of policy that are handled every day.

And so to business. First, two or three words. In Greek, the eschaton is the blessed Last Day, hoped for at the end of history; and *ta eschata* are the Last Things. In Latin Christianity, these Last Things are traditionally Death, (the Last) Judgement,

Heaven, and Hell. Eschatology is then the theory of, or an account of, the Last Things, which are usually felt to be threatening and getting closer to us. The Four Horsemen of the Apocalypse is a phrase derived from Revelation, chapter 6, an unclear passage about the opening of the seven seals. The fourth and most important horseman is Death on a pale horse; the others are War, Famine and Pestilence. They are the woes that may be unleashed against those who attract God's wrath by major violations of the divine order.

The New Testament book that tells of these things is called, very inaccurately in common speech, Revelations. Its Greek title is simply *Apokalypsis Ioannou*, the "Apocalypse of John". The words *apocalypse* and *revelation* both mean, quite straightforwardly, "unveiling", or "the drawing back of a curtain". Thus the writer of an apocalypse is one who is helpfully drawing back the curtain of ignorance that hides future events from our eyes. He has been vouchsafed a vision of what is going to happen. It is confusing that in modern English *apocalyptic* has come to mean "referring to the complete and final destruction of the world".

Another much-abused word in this area is *holocaust*. In the Septuagint, the Greek version of the Hebrew Bible, a *holocaust* is a whole burnt offering. The gods, up in the heavens, used to lean over and enjoy the stink of the burning meat rising from the altars below them on Earth. Later, the word was transferred to the massacre of the Jews in the Nazi period, as an attempt to make bittersweet grim poetry of the gas ovens. It is never a word to use at all lightly.

In general, my policy is always to prefer the original technical use of words like "deconstruction" and "food chain"; and the original etymological use of terms like "decimation" and "anticipation". I need to make this announcement here, because in this essay we cannot avoid wandering back and forth across the frontiers between religious, philosophical, and scientific thought.

To reduce ambiguity, and to help the reader to interpret what I'm saying, I have to be somewhat of a pedant. But if I can be understood as having, over the past thirty-five years, always used the terms "realism" and "non-realism" in the philosophical sense, and *not* in the ordinary language sense, then I have a slightly better chance of one day being understood. Pedantry it has to be then, and don't get me even started on the subject of "the elephant in the room".[11]

To return to our present topic, early modern physics after Galileo viewed the world as if from the point of view of an imaginary blind mathematician, who is presented with a great many measurements, and some general ideas about body, space, time, and motion. He tries by thought experiments to conjure up a diagram or working model of the realm that is marked out, or perhaps presupposed, by all the measurements. God, Galileo thinks to himself, is a mathematician and engineer. His thinking-up of it all coincides with and just is his creating of it, and the finite, human mathematician-engineer tries to track God's mathematical reasoning and so to understand the structure of the world that God has established.

In early modern physics, as launched by Galileo, the world is thus a machine whose workings can be completely described by invoking only definitions of *matter* as occupied space, of *motion*, and mathematical *laws of motion*. The world-machine is a rather abstract working model thought up by an almost equally abstract mathematical physicist, who sees the world-machine from no particular point of view. His body is doubtless taken to be a part of the world-machine; but his mind, his sense perception of the world from a finite human point of view, and his agency are *not*.

This early modern physics, when perfected by Newton, was very speedily recognized as one of the greatest human intellectual achievements. It can easily be used to calculate accurately the motions of larger bodies of every kind, from planets to bullets. It was used to calculate the paths of the space vehicles of the

1960s. But it creates intellectual puzzles that have never entirely gone away.

The main one—still a fascinating puzzle—has to do with the relation between God's mind, the human mind, and empirical existence. In God's infinite mind, the whole history of nature is posited and completely understood through the laws of nature that God's reason ordains. There is no need to draw any distinction between the total world-plan in God's mind, and the actual, empirical existence of the world outside God's mind. When God makes something, he does not separate it from his own mind. Nothing ever is outside the divine mind. God is an idealist.[12] His mind has no outside.

The human physicist, however, is in a somewhat different position. A human is not God, and the human mind is finite. When humans do classical physics, they *think* the world-order in the same way as God does (that is, mathematically), but their thinking is not *creative* in the way that God's is. So human physicists' total world-picture cannot quite coincide with the world's actual existence. In which case, *what is the difference* between human physicists' very big and complex mathematical world-model, and that world's actual empirical existence?

We now reword the question. What's the difference between a complete, *really* complete, mathematical physicist's description of the world, and the world's actual existence? What's the extra? Empirical existence? OK: let's include that in the complete description. No: surely one cannot simply *define* something into existence. In which case, empirical existence—there happening to be something out there to which the complete description applies—will have to be located outside language. Empirical contingent happening-to-be will have to be located out in the mysterious ineffable real world, on the far side of our language about it. Which is very odd, because it sounds as if we are attempting to say *both* that early modern physics *can* describe the empirical world and that it *cannot*! No wonder that Blaise Pascal's reaction to the new physics was one of puzzlement and alienation. The old religious world-picture made you feel at home in the world. The new and vastly superior physics makes us feel like lost souls.

Newton's physics described a mechanistic universe, orderly and harmonious. Each planet's path was the product of two forces, the centrifugal force pressing it to fly away out of its orbit and the centripetal force of gravity simultaneously pulling it back towards the sun. So the planetary orbits seemed to be proved mathematically, and the whole system sang. But it said nothing about purposiveness or values. Its perfection was very frosty.

Newton's prestige was so great that after him anybody with scientific pretensions more or less *had* to follow his method. The results could be surprising. T. R. Malthus, also a Cambridge man and a cleric, produced in *The Principle of Population* (1798–1803), the first work of modern social science. He noted that in new countries such as the United States and Australia, land was relatively abundant and the population could increase very rapidly. But in relatively mature countries such as those of Europe, population was more nearly stable, because there was little scope for further increasing the amount of land under cultivation. So Malthus argues, along highly Newtonian lines, that in a fully mature country human numbers will be stabilized, as the human desire for increase of population comes up against various implacable checks—severe competition for the finite available resources, plague, famine and war. In short, precisely the Four Horsemen of the Apocalypse!

In Malthus, eschatology returns within the world-view of a Christian who accepts Newton's notion of cosmic stability as the outcome of an interplay of conflicting forces. God has designed a very cunning system: control your own reproductive urge, or the workings of the world-system will do it for you. The choice is between moral self-restraint and very painful limitation of your numbers by the operation of implacable external checks.

A generation later, the young Charles Darwin read Malthus very closely. Darwin was another orthodox Newtonian who thought that the system of nature remains relatively stable because it is produced by the interplay of conflicting forces. Like Malthus, he noted that not only humans, but all or most biological species can—and if they get the chance, *will*—reproduce themselves very rapidly; but in practice their numbers are checked by their own struggle for existence against each other for food, and against predators and disease. As in Malthus' argument, the whole system is in its outcome benign, because what theologians call "the problem of evil" has a functional role within a system which, taken as a whole, works to improve the adaptation of each species to its environment.

Darwin ends his book on an optimistic note: "We can look forward to a secure future of great length", as the operation of natural selection makes each species gradually better and better adapted to its environment. Many readers have noted that *The Origin of Species* is the last major scientific work that keeps (in its first edition) a reference to God, as having presumably been the creator of the very first living beings. But few people notice what a remarkable synthesis of different themes Darwin has achieved. The archaic human belief in the beauty and the harmonious order of nature; the Newtonian doctrine that nature's stable order is the product of an interplay of opposed forces; the instrumental role of strict moral discipline and environmental limits (including evils and suffering) in keeping all species beautifully adapted to their environment; *and* the nineteenth-century optimism that hoped for steady general improvement without undue violence, and within a harmonious and self-maintaining order. Darwin is keeping all these balls in the air at once.

Nineteenth-century scientific thought, it seems, still tried to be orthodox Newtonian. But as its attention turned to geology, to biology, and to human society, it could no longer limit itself to laying down "mathematical principles of natural philosophy".[13] Living things, with their *interest* in life, and human beings as moral agents, were now part of the picture. We were no longer alienated from nature; on the contrary, we had become thoroughly embedded into it and interwoven with it. We even feel ourselves akin to it and *responsible* for it. And all this makes a certain return of eschatology inevitable. From the seventeenth century the new mechanistic physics had military and engineering applications. It was a tool of *power*, a power that might be misused with very serious consequences. Today, our newer *biological* science urges us to conserve the living world that is our home too.

Western countries perhaps rightly regard modern science as their greatest cultural achievement. But we should not regard "science" as the name of a single distinctive method and attitude to the world. On the contrary, the fascination of the history of ideas in the West lies in the fact that from the first our science had various strands in it, mathematical, experimental, aesthetic, moral, religious, and political. It has been a complex and argumentative cultural movement, and it's got a long way to go yet. And do not assume that those who struggle to conserve, nature, and who warn us about climate change are somehow being unscientific types who preach boring sermons.

# 6

# On Not Going Anywhere

## Learning to Live without Any Supporting Narrative

A century ago, a stream of European migrants were still landing in a New York that was poor, shabby, and very hard-working: a city still building itself. They were fleeing European poverty and discrimination, and hoping for a better life. In practice, such first-generation Americans often had a very hard time indeed, but they endured it because they believed and hoped that their children would have a better life. As, of course, they usually did.

A little story about a better future: this is a minimal example of the kind of small consolatory narrative by which in the past millions of lives have been made bearable.

Now consider an even simpler example. I buy a new-generation mobile phone from Apple or Samsung because I believe that it will be a little better than the previous one. Indeed, we all of us normally expect almost all products to be slowly but continuously improved. The newer mobile phone will be better designed, slimmer, more elegant and more efficient. It will do more things. Without that expectation of continuous product improvement, how would we ever be persuaded to buy anything new? In Eastern Europe, during the two generations after World War Two, factories produced quotas of products as directed by the ruling communist party bodies. Improvement stopped, design stopped—and around 1990 the entire system suddenly died of boredom.

Since the early nineteenth century, many commentators have suggested that the distinctive features of Western culture, which have given to it its energy and its huge success, are a touch of dissatisfaction with present reality, coupled with a firm belief that things can be made to be better in the future than they are today. Individuals need to have scraps of narrative in their heads and in their everyday speech that help to keep them going. Without that belief, they might run into both *population* decline and severe *economic* decline.

At the opposite extreme, several of the more ancient of the principal world faiths have very large-scale narratives of cosmic creation, fall and redemption. Displayed in mosaic in St. Mark's, Venice; in stained glass at Chartres; and in a cycle of popular dramas at York in the English mystery plays, the Christian grand narrative was once known to everyone in Christian countries. It told you your place in the whole scheme of things, and lasted until the nineteenth century in Britain, where schoolchildren still learned the list of kings and queens of England for patriotic over a century of the second law of thermodynamics. Entropy increases, until no hotspots remain, and the universe becomes uniformly thinly scattered and very cold. This was popularly called "the heat-death of the Universe", a state in which there will be nothing it all except an immeasurable ocean of radiation. As Keynes once put it: "In the long run we're all dead." That much is still true, on standard physical theory. But from the 1930s onwards new worries surface. Philosophers such as Heidegger begin to be suspicious of the destructive power both of modern technology, and behind it, of the modern technological mind-set which sees everything as raw material, ready-to-hand, and ripe for exploitation. After World War Two, and in particular after Hiroshima, there came also the first of a long series of scares about the destructive effects of human activities upon the natural environment. In a few cases, a scare about chemical pollution—by DDT, for example, or chloroflourocarbons in the upper atmosphere, or progesterone accumulating in our water—could easily be ended by simply discontinuing the use of the chemical in question. Other issues have proved more intractable. Population and resource exhaustion have been prominent amongst them: it seemed that we might simply run out of oil, and be unable to feed such vast numbers of people. In many parts of the world, land once fertile had become desert. By the 1970s it was clear that growth could not go on forever. On the contrary, it was already understood that it was impossible for the whole human race to live for long at the American level of consumption. In which case a plateau was being reached, and to avoid long-term decline we needed to start concentrating upon changing over to a sustainable pattern of consumption and way of life. Then during the late 1970s amongst a few younger scientists there began to be talk of the greenhouse effect and global warming. I recall being instructed in these ideas by friends and young colleagues during the 1970s.[16] A decade later, I recall being told by an American scientist friend that, at the behest of the big Texan oilmen, the Reagan Administration had stopped funding research into methods of "cleanly" capturing solar energy, so that we could use it as plants do but perhaps more efficiently, to trap carbon dioxide and turn it into food.

Since the late 1980s the old belief that population growth will slow and stabilize as the planet becomes more crowded has returned. The United Nations currently expects stability at about ten billion by the middle of the present century. But ever-growing life expectancy will continue to fuel overall population growth for at least some while yet, and both India and China have learnt by painful experience how very hard it is to hold down the birth rate by political means. And even if the overall world population *does* stabilize at ten billion, we'll be puzzled to feed so many people without much use of genetically modified crops, which remain widely unpopular.

The upshot of all this is that since the late 1980s the greenhouse effect, successively renamed "global warming" and "climate change", has become and now remains our biggest single anxiety. The most tangible and familiar evidence of global warming is the much-publicized melting of ice at the Poles, and in the Himalayas. Another small but striking piece of evidence is the sight of French vineyard owners surveying the South Downs in Kent and Sussex, looking for the sites on which they will produce the champagne of the future. Or take, for example, the fact that a butterfly enthusiast can tell you exactly how much further north each year the Comma butterfly is moving its range. Climate change is becoming built into the way we interpret a wide range of issues. We know it's happening, and by having successfully persuaded us to do far too little about it, the army of climate change deniers have made it now unstoppable. There is no longer even very much public alarm. It is too familiar and too big an issue to think clearly about. During the Tony Blair years a very able civil servant, Nicholas Stern, was commissioned to prepare a report to the United Kingdom government on the practicalities and the economics of combatting climate change. Reporting in 2008 (see p. 107f. below), Stern found that it was still possible for one country to deal with the problem at tolerable cost. But getting all the other countries to do the same things during the same period was of course a much trickier matter, and now the years have slipped by, little has been done, world fossil-fuel burning is still rising, and it may be too late to save many of the world's low-lying coastal cities and settlements.

Given this general background, extending from the 1930s to Lord Stern's report (2008), what date shall we assign to the beginning of humanity's last days? Geologists seem to be settling upon the year 1610 for the beginning of the Anthropocene epoch. That is an early date, and in approximate parallel with it I will propose 1973 as the beginning of the human *Eschaton*. In about 1973 observers began to say: We have reached the top of the hill. It cannot go on like this. From now on we will have done very well if we can reach sustainability. We'll need to use scientific and technological advances to hold back, and even considerably, to *reduce* our consumption of fossil fuel energy and must learn to do so without serious cultural and economic decline. By looking at the case of computers since the Apollo programme we can see how it may be possible in future to do more and more with less and less. We may be able to get by: but nobody likes the thought of wholly giving up the traditional ideas of continual progressive betterment. And we *certainly* don't want to see children, or air travel, being strictly rationed.

How are we to live within such limits as I have been describing? I use the word "ethics" to describe a general "spirituality", or ethical-religious policy and philosophy of life, preferring to reserve the word "morality" for codes of behavioural rules. So here I am talking about a general way of relating oneself to life, when I use the word "ethic". And note that because of my age, I am in my own last days, as well as recognizing that there is also a sense of which we may all of us be already in the last days of humanity. I am a Christian of sorts, but so modern and rationalist that I have no expectation of life after death. My whole outlook is now presentist and short-term. I just cannot consider the possibility of any long-term personal future. So I follow the advice of Jesus, and simply do not think about tomorrow. I live for the day, as extravertively as I can, and try to be as generous and life-affirming as I can whilst I remain alive. And I am suggesting that it is appropriate for all of us to shift our ethical outlook in the same "solar" direction. If the future is dark, live hard now, while you can.

As things get tougher over the next three or four decades, we will see more and more of things that are already familiar: states fail and peaceful government is replaced by predatory militias; ordinary social morality breaks down, and society collapses into wandering gangs of desperate refugees, economic migrants, and boat people. The super-rich vanish into their remote, fortified cruise ships and other hideaways. Military-minded survivalists try to create small local dictatorships.

Against a background of this type, in morality we should try not ever to join either the super-rich who have opted out, or the wandering tribes. We should cling for as long as we possibly can to something like decent government and to a society that is fraternal, interdependent and mutually supporting. We try to maintain communal production and allocation of food, shelter and so on, and communal collection and preservation of what remains of the old culture. We try to keep going a minimal conception of man as being through-and-through a social being, and we battle to keep education and literacy.

Those who insist upon trying to maintain a human political minimum will undoubtedly be threatened by wandering beggars, robbers, and militias. We should not fight them. We should try as hard as we can to welcome them, to assimilate them, and to convert them to our project. If we can do this, the hard times that are probably ahead may see the forging of the long awaited

# 7

# The Coherence of Life and Culture

For millions of years the main hominid line developed slowly, at the gentle pace usual in biological evolution. Then gradually, with the slow development of language came the beginnings of culture: culture acquired, accumulated, and transmitted, culture bringing with it real advantage and something of the intoxication of power. Our ancestors began to change over from biology-led development to culture-led development. In due course, the pace of development began to quicken. Whereas in tradition-directed societies innovation is usually reckoned to be deplorable and probably sinful, we gradually moved over to an enlightened type of mentality which criticizes supposedly "holy"

tradition and instead demands constant progressive innovation and improvement.

The gradual acceleration of human cultural development was not uniform. Some great and enduring civilizations of the Bronze Age were very slow-moving: in ancient Egypt the art style changed so slowly that artefacts are often difficult for a non-specialist to date. China too was often in no great hurry, as for example in the period we in the West think of as the early Middle Ages. But then towards the end of the Middle Ages—in what we may think of as the early Tudor period—a spirit of active curiosity about the wider world stirred in England (Richard Hakluyt's *Voyages*), Portugal (Vasco da Gama and Magellan), and Holland. The great navigators mapped coastlines, and began to fill in the map of the world. It is true that in the same period China was rich and powerful, and Chinese merchant ships also found their way around much of the world. But in China they did not have learned Geographical Societies at home, which appraised, collected and published the new discoveries. The West *did* have the machinery for gathering, checking out, systematizing and accumulating new knowledge; and it is that machinery that made and still makes all the difference.

There were already a number of these peer-group scientific societies in Galileo's Italy and Descartes' Paris. But the foremost of them was—and perhaps still is—The Royal Society of London for the Improvement of Natural Knowledge, founded 1660, incorporated 1662, and enjoying the patronage of the government ever since. From 1662 we can date the dawning realization that modern civilization is based upon *knowledge*, and in particular *scientific* knowledge. Continual production of new knowledge is expected, and a whole range of learned societies and journals are constantly engaged in gathering, reviewing, systematizing and publishing new knowledge.

I mention all this in order to make one important point. Individual scientists occasionally make a new observation, as when the astrophysicist Jocelyn Burnell observed a pulsar. But such straightforward discoveries are not the most important events in the history of science. The most important event occurs when a gifted individual finds and proposes a large-scale organizing theory that makes sense of a whole area of knowledge. Two very famous examples are, first, D. I. Mendeleev's Periodic Table of the Elements which more than any other theory makes sense of much of inorganic chemistry. It is so good a theory that Mendeleev himself derived successful predictions about as-yet-undiscovered elements from it. A second example is D. P. McKenzie's theory of the earth's crust as being made up of a number of very large tectonic plates, which move slowly around, floating on the currents of molten rock that underlie them. Their movement, sometimes pulling apart and sometimes colliding, gives us the history of the continents, the locations of earthquakes, the production of great mountain ranges, and so on. The theory, once pointed out, is so obviously good and useful that much detail was quickly filled in by others, and soon the theory seemed to be what we have always thought. It provides a coherent geological story that helps to make sense of the subject as a whole.[17]

My present point is that it is these big organizing ideas that give to scientific knowledge its huge power and authority. The most famous of them were proposed by Sir Isaac Newton, Charles Darwin, and Albert Einstein, but for my present purpose it was more illuminating to take examples less familiar to the general public—including a geological idea that was put forward only about forty-five years ago. It helps to remind us that our civilization is science-based; it rests upon a far bigger and stronger foundation of knowledge than any previous society has had. Beginning with the establishment of the Royal Society (1660–62), it has, since about the time of Lavoisier and the French Revolution, produced a steadily accelerating torrent of cultural change. Today, it is faster than ever. When I was young we used to marvel at the American energy that took people from the first powered flight to the moon landings in just over sixty years; but the development of computers and all the associated communication and information technologies since the 1960s has perhaps been even faster. Consider the huge enthusiasm with which ordinary, poor, and not well educated people everywhere have seized upon the new gadgets and have learnt to operate them. Nowadays almost all of humanity is in flight from tradition, and eagerly embraces innovation.

Another modern example is the cultural after effects of the early 1950s announcement of the double-helix structure of DNA by Crick and Watson. Over the decades since, their announcement has led to a great proliferation of new knowledge over the whole range of the life sciences and medical sciences, with applications that range from the detection of criminals to the design of pharmaceuticals.

All this hugely rapid growth in knowledge and in the new technologies that come with it leads the optimists to entertain fantasies of power. People begin to think that almost any disease can be conquered and any problem solved by funding sufficient research. We are rapidly extending our expectation of life: are we not now very close to finding the genes that cause ageing, and so to deferring death for many more decades? As for worries about our earthly environment, when they start to become really urgent in two generations' time or so, are we not sure to be able to find a technological remedy? Some very fancy possibilities are already being discussed.

Pessimists are unimpressed by all this. They are shocked by the still-continuing acceleration of scientific and technological growth and power. They think of the tarantella, and of farce: of a whirling frenzy that gets faster and faster until it suddenly and violently crashes. We are already seeing more extreme weather events, and with them we are also seeing extreme forms of moral breakdown, reactionary religious fanaticism, and the failure of the state in country after country. As the pessimists see it, the collapse of our science-based industrial civilization has already begun, even while in the northeastern states of the United States and in California it is still racing ahead.

The strongest argument the pessimists can adduce is that there has so far been no high-quality religious response to our situation at all. The moderate religion praised by politicians is stone dead. Take for example, the case of Islam, which is widely regarded as the world religion in which faith remains most vigorous. In the past, Islam produced magnificent architecture, high-quality philosophical theology, and much fine poetry and mystical writing. What is there today? Who can point to more than a tiny handful of books since the 1950s, attempting a modern Islamic philosophical theology? There is no modern critical study of the Qur'an at all. I do not know of any really good contemporary Islamic poetry or mysticism. There is some very good cinema in Iran, and there are also some Sufis, but they are attacked by their own co-religionists. As for Islam's once-glorious architecture, I had better say nothing at all about the buildings that have recently been erected at Mecca.

Today, we face the probability that within a century humankind will move into a period of global disaster vastly greater in scale than the small and local world wars of the early twentieth century. Many, many novelists and filmmakers have tried to imagine it and to prepare us for it (*The Road, Ridley Walker, Memoirs of a Survivor*). But there has been and still is no serious religious and ethical response at all. I believe that before Pope Francis issued his recent Encyclical, the religious leader most keen on green issues was Bartholomew I, Patriarch of Constantinople, but no text by him seems to be available. The Catholic theologian Hans Küng did once announce that he proposed to devote the remainder of his life to environmental issues, but he has not produced anything comparable with his big earlier books of popular theology.

We must hope that Pope Francis has the time and the strength to build upon his own recent initiative in this area.

Why is religion currently failing so badly? What we nowadays call the world religions are the remains of what were once great religion-based civilizations, which produced architecture, sculpture, painting, manuscripts, and, of course, religious societies and religious lives. Looking back with our hindsight, it appears today that in each major faith the great tradition ended between 150 and 300 years ago. Today, all that is left of each faith is a heritage appreciation society, nostalgically recalling its own past, but no longer capable of adding anything important to it. Serious religious thought seems not to exist at all.

This is a very serious matter. I have suggested that in a branch of natural science, a single big organising idea, such as tectonic plate theory in geology, or biological evolution, may join up and give coherence to the entire subject. Rather similarly, it should be the job of big religious narratives and ideas to make sense of our life and hold together the entire culture. But in our society, religion is old and no longer intellectually vigorous enough to do that job. But if we cannot produce a strong religious response to our growing environmental crisis we shall be at risk of general cultural disintegration and social breakdown. And that is the present position. Some hard-headed types think that the decline of religion during the past two or three centuries is a good thing, and will not have any unfortunate consequences. They are wrong. We need not just a green technical fix but a total, life-centred green religion, or a green refurbishment of one of our old faiths.

We therefore find ourselves obliged to invent an ethical and religious response to the fast-approaching final collapse of our civilization. I have already suggested that in the case of Christianity by far the most precious residue that remains to us after the end of the great tradition in about 1725 is the tradition of humanitarian ethics that derives ultimately from the early Jesus, and still has great influence around the world—for example, in the medical and related professions, and the big international aid organizations. Those of us who have been deeply touched by that ethic cannot possibly respond to the coming eschaton by withdrawing, as the rich will, into well supplied and defended fortresses. But nor can we simply join the wandering bands of refugees and militias that will be the only option for ordinary people. Our preference will be to struggle for as long as we possibly can to keep alive the idea of a generous, open, undefended, and free society, which—like the early United States—is generous enough to welcome poor incomers, and try to find places for them. We have to cling to the values that make human life worthwhile, and we would rather die than be reduced to a desperate struggle against other destitute people for the last few bullets and tins of baked beans left amongst the ruins.

In a few countries the state has already collapsed. The streets are infested with gunmen, and ordinary people's lives have become a struggle to maintain shelter and a few daily scraps of food. We must not accept that. We must actively argue with the gunmen for a generous society, for non-violence, and for humanitarian values.

What of the religious life, in an age when we will no longer be able to choose a career, a planned life with a teleological (goal-seeking) life story? Interestingly, in the old order there was already something called "the religious life", in which people dropped out of narrative, out of history and out of ordinary social life. Their life no longer had a worldly purpose. And I can well imagine that in the future people of talent who wish to dedicate themselves to social care and cultural production may revive the idea of the religious life. It is already the case, especially for women who have high talent and a strong intellectual or artistic vocation, that they find it well-nigh impossible to reconcile the claims of their work with the demands of children and domestic life.[18] We should not and do not advocate any revival of the ideal of chastity or celibacy, but one can well imagine that in very harsh future conditions people who have some special talent and a sense of vocation will choose to remain childless for life. Some have already taken this path.

Similarly in the harsh conditions of the future there will be people who revive the traditional idea of poverty, by living as far as possible without any possessions. Today in the West even ordinary working people typically may consume more food, clothing, and energy than they need. We should learn to consume less, noting that the new technologies make it easy to store prodigious amounts of data—including, for example, thousands of books—in a very small handheld device. There is no doubt that very much lower consumption is technologically possible and environmentally highly desirable. So we should make a virtue of it. Even such practices as learning by heart a considerable amount of great poetry can be highly enriching. I personally have done it to beguile periods of poor health.

It may be thought that in the hard times ahead people will not have time or even inclination to think of high culture and the contemplative virtues. During the Bronze Age, and again in the Iron Age, early city-dwellers in the Old World were often plagued by the breakdown of the state and of all central authority. People lived through bad periods, the times of Warring States in China, India, Mesopotamia and Egypt. In Europe we recall our own dark times after the Fall of the (Western) Roman Empire, and no doubt these recollections have influenced the modern novelists who have tried to imagine the life of our descendants, a century or so from now. Small bands of shabby, hungry survivors wander across a ruined, burnt-out landscape searching for any remains of food. They are in constant fear of armed gangs, and—to some extent—also of each other. It is the world of the Four Horsemen of the Apocalypse, and I suggest that it will be a world in which ordinary people will need a religious discipline like that of the

Buddhist *sangha* to help people to calm their violent passions and to think rationally about how best to live.

In many parts of the Middle East and of Africa the conditions of life for many ordinary people are already pretty much as described by the novelists I have quoted. The catastrophe has occurred, the state has broken down, the regular distribution of food and the circulation of money has broken down, and people live from hand to mouth amongst the ruins. In such a world people easily become prematurely aged, and worn-out with anxiety. Meditation can be wonderfully refreshing and restful. It can help us to live without any purpose or 'meaning' in life: it can show us how we can get by without a Big Story, and without heavy consumption. In the short run, we are just trudging on, but in the longer run we are looking for a possibility of reestablishing some form of farming and settled life. The Israeli kibbutz is a good model, and it may be a type of community in which urbanised people may learn to go back to the land.

"God"? For the present we do not need to think of returning to any notion of almighty power. Isn't that (that is, the love of almighty power) what has brought the human race to its present dire straights? If anyone brings up the subject of God, we shall give an ethical answer: "Love is God". Love and love alone is "the ethical supernatural" which can give meaning and value to life. While we can still feel it, we will be able to live on for a while.

# 8

# After Humanity

Alfred Tennyson foresaw that man, like all other animal species, was destined to end up sealed into the fossil record. He did not care for the prospect: it seemed to him to mean that our existence on Earth was pointless, a brief and trivial episode that will in the end mean nothing to anyone, for there will be nobody around for it to mean anything *to*.

A biologist friend of mine was more cheerful. He hated what humans have done to the whole biosphere, and expected that after the extinction of man the earth would quickly begin to heal. New species would soon evolve to replace those we are currently losing, and in a few million years the planet will be as beautiful as ever. "But—to whom?" I interjected, because of my conviction that every world needs a knowing conscious subject whose world it is, just as all subjects need a world which can function for them as the theatre in which they enact or present their self-hood.[19] The world and the self belong together: you cannot have the one without the other, and the thought of a world without any subject whose world it is, who calls it his or her home, is a non-thought which we shouldn't entertain, and from which we cannot derive any consolation.

My biologist friend was quite unimpressed. He loves the earth, the biosphere, much more than he loves himself or any of his own kind. Like most scientists he is reluctant to examine the scientific observer and theorist, the subject whom his own language always presupposes; and besides, scientists don't like philosophy. In the person of Aristotle and his teaching, philosophy was the subject they had had to conquer in order to get the whole mighty engine of modern science rolling.

I persisted, arguing that scientists are inconsistent in welcoming the Death of God the Creator, whilst at the same time wanting to keep the creation as a ready-made law-governed real world for science to study, a fully furnished working home that was all ready and waiting for the first human couple to be inserted into it. And notice too that in the Genesis myth Adam and Eve do not begin life as babies. They are created as adults who have somehow already learned a language, and are already *educated*, but have no personal histories and no memories. (Eve can have had no memory of consenting to be Adam's mate, a point for feminists!) They are also surprisingly clean, and (in Christian art) are fresh from the hairdresser. Masaccio has one of the very few scruffy Eves.

My biologist friend obviously did not believe any of that nonsense. He was well aware that the earliest humans all had an animal ancestry, all began as babies, and all began with a consciousness, which was at first no more than a disorderly tumult of sensations and feelings. No more than that is given—even today, to us adults. But then somehow, through their developing communication with each other, these early humans slowly learned to build their first picture of a common world in which they lived together the life of a human group. And they had to do it all without any extraneous help. They had to do it purely immanently, from within their own early human point of view. They never heard from anybody outside themselves who might see where they were going wrong, and gently correct them. No: they had to do it entirely unaided and uncorrected. They were not in any position to draw any distinction between *our* world and *the* world. For them, *our* world was in effect *the* world, and their picture of "our-world", as they might have called it, was true insofar as they themselves had made it out of what they had found to be pragmatically true *for them*.

Thus I was arguing that we humans, being on our own, cannot help but be somewhat anthropocentric. We, and we only, have evolved all our various world-pictures, religions and philosophies amongst ourselves, and entirely from inside our own selves. Of all of them it can be said that, if they work for the people who use them, then they are true. When we were thinking about the first humans just now, we were imaginatively putting ourselves alongside them, and very much wishing to help them a little. But no, they did not have anybody there for them, and we must remember that they really were on their own, and had nothing to build their world *out of* but their own language and their own experience. We alone invented all the ordinary natural languages, and all the supplementary sign-systems of music, mathematics and roads. It follows that science does not give us dogmatic truth about *the* world, but only highly refined pragmatic truth about *our* world that is enough for us to go on, for now.

Now we begin to move away from my biologist, who is getting restless about my denial of matter and objectivity. In the Middle Ages, Westerners thought of all that was real under three great headings: the created world, the human soul, and

God. God was self-existent, the most real being and the other two were his creatures. Then the history of Western thought from the Renaissance to Nietzsche is the history of the slow and much-disputed replacement of this scheme by another, in which everything comes to be seen only from the human point of view, and in which there are now just two great topics: there is the disorderly flux of experience, and there is the motion of language, ceaselessly trying to pin it down, shape it, find patterns in it and make something of it. From within the ceaseless buzz of language there gradually emerges awareness of myself as a speaker, of other selves as my interlocutors and my kinsfolk, and of my own life as a lengthy stream of language-formed events, interwoven with the events of other lives.

All along, we have never been able to step out of our own only-human perspective; but as the world-picture of ordinary language develops, we begin to notice oddities and irregularities within it which call for special explanation. Science develops as a collection of supplementary vocabularies and bodies of theory, which make intelligible and predictable a range of events, which had seemed anomalous and alarming. But science never jumps altogether clear of ordinary language, which is the nearest thing to something truly foundational that we have. And science by its very nature is always restless and dissatisfied, trying to improve current theory.

Because it lays such emphasis upon *public* methods of testing the adequacy of its theories, science is a strongly *communal* enterprise. Possessing a large body of committed professionals has given science today much more public authority than either of its old rivals, religion or philosophy, can ever now hope to regain. Thus in the English-speaking world, it is the *scientists* whose expert testimonies are readily accepted by the lawcourts. Compared with them, the rest of us are nowhere. I have ventured to point out that Descartes and a few like him would have done better *not* to emulate the theologians by claiming something like *dogmatic* truth for their theories. Science's unmatched strength lies not in its dogmatic rigidity, but in its flexibility and its ready openness to revision and correction.

It is, furthermore, entirely understandable that scientists professionally concerned with studying the worlds of geology and biology should develop a great love of their subject-matter, and should deplore the massive extinction event that human activities have already triggered off. Our hunger, especially for food, is already turning vast areas of the land and the oceans into lifeless near-desert. And I further understand that scientists may wish to cast their message in the form of a conditional threat of doom: "If we carry on like this, we will destroy ourselves". That's correct. It is also quite probably correct that we'll never be able to get international agreements sufficiently strong to prevent disaster; and it is also correct that green technology and the like, which enjoin us to take good care of our bees and whales, are not an adequate religious response to what is coming upon us.

What would be an *adequate* religious response to our current environmental worries? To answer that question, we must begin by observing that a truly heartfelt *religious* response is always highly self-involving. With that in mind, we can now set out the answer in a series of sentences:

1. In the past it was believed that the world out there was created by God. But today it appears that *we* are the only world-builders. We created all the language, and we are the only theorists. Truth in science is not discovered: it's *made* by us. The world around us is always *our* world, built by us according to rules laid down by us. It is a home for us, it meets our needs, it *works* for us, and it reflects our feelings—and also our faults. Crudely, but truthfully, we should acknowledge that our world, of which we are part, is a judgement upon ourselves. Beautiful, but also botched. Sometimes self-destructive, as we are.

2. If we perceive that our world is going badly wrong, that'll be because there is much wrong with ourselves—and in particular with our greedy, exploitative use of our technologies and our lust for power. Governments in particular have always subsidized science for the sake of its military spin-off. So if the world is going badly wrong, even to the point of destruction, we need to change what ordinary people speak of as "our whole attitude to life"—that is, our religious orientation.

3. According to Karl Marx, the task of a critical philosophy like his own is not just to interpret the world, but to change it. And to change the world, Marx maintained, we must get ourselves organized and overthrow the ruling class, which presently controls the shaping of reality. Marxism-Leninism then prescribed how that is to be done. But unfortunately this policy merely replaced one ruling class with another which turned out to be no better. As the unforgettable Czech joke had it: "Capitalism is a system for the exploitation of man by man; but under communism it is the other way round." Marx was right to see that in the philosophy of the future the primacy of practice and expression will need to replace the old primacy of theoretical contemplation. But the primacy of ethics as I understand it is the primacy of changing the self and its orientation towards life. We need to become solar. We need to free ourselves from all forms of ressentiment, and learn how to love life and to live generously. If we can pause a while in our rush to expend all available natural resources, and instead learn how to live by expending *ourselves*, we may find ourselves becoming fit to inhabit this earth for a while longer yet.

This brief sketch has indicated why I now put ethics before ontology, and the good before being. It also indicates why my approach to ethics is emotivist and *not* realist. Ethics begins at the end of the world; that is, with a sudden appreciation of the utter contingency and transience of our life. Everything is passing away all the time, and there is not anything out there on which we can lean and from which we can derive the values or the law by which we are to live. We have instead to find a new solar, expressive way of living purely affirmatively, living by love.

# 9

# Eschatology, Globalized and Personalized

Eschatological belief has now become completely secularized. In the years immediately after World War Two Herbert Butterfield, a Professor of History at Cambridge and a Methodist layman, published an essay under the title *Christianity and History*, in which he indicated that we could discern the Hand of God, Divine Judgment, and "the working-out of a moral Providence in history" in the ruin of Nazi Germany and the fates of Mussolini and Hitler.[20] I was surprised even then, for history—even *church* history—has surely been a secular subject since the days of Hume and Gibbon. Indeed, "sacred letters" and "human letters" have been separated in University syllabuses ever since the first Protestant attempts to redesign the map of learning.

The Roman Empire as studied by Classics students did not take any cognisance at all of Christian origins, and Christianity was noticed only as its products and doings became publicly significant. Thus Protestantism from the first seemed to take a tacitly non-realist view of Christianity's claims about its own origins.[21] They did not merit serious consideration: they were a matter of "faith".

Today history is secular, and it is hard to think of any supernatural claim that has recently been taken seriously—or could nowadays *ever* be taken seriously. When I was young newspapers reported the annual pilgrimage to Lourdes as if they still thought there was merit in the ordinary believers' notion that after the doctors have failed one might in desperation turn to the supernatural world in the hope of miraculous healing. But today even senior churchmen joke about the idea that beyond the powers and resources of modern science-based medicine there is a further realm of supernatural diagnoses and healings, in which candidates for sainthood must "do their practicals", if they are to be approved for canonization.

With the general final secularization of Western thought since the 1960s, almost the whole of the old eschatology has vanished. One no longer hears anything about the Second Coming, the Last Trump, and the Day of Judgment. On the evidence of contemporary funeral services the beliefs in the old "particular judgment" of the individual after death and her or his consignment to purgatory have also completely disappeared. After death nothing further happens, or can happen, to us.

It is true that journalists still describe Christian fundamentalists as being traditionalists. But on the evidence of their own language the conservative evangelicals and others like them are *not* true traditionalists who think it important to preserve the whole of traditional faith intact. On the contrary, they have themselves already quietly abandoned large areas of traditional belief. (If you doubt me, try asking them whether a Christian should have, or need, insurance coverage; where unbaptised babies who die end up; or why we pray for some things and not for others. And do they really think a cancer diagnosis is a divine visitation that calls for repentance?

Today, then, the old supernatural eschatology is secularized; but it has not simply vanished. The old feeling that our time is running out, that life is short, that a great dark cloud hangs over us, and that we should consider changing our lives before it is too late—all this has since 1945 repeatedly returned to us in new and secular forms.

Why? Because Western culture after only about three centuries of furiously accelerating growth in knowledge, technology, population, wealth, and world power had suddenly crashed so violently—Germany's Nazi period being the most terrible event in the whole history of the West, taking place in the area of Europe which had seen the highest cultural achievements of all.[22] Mozart, Goethe, and Beethoven; Nietzsche, Freud, and Einstein: many of Europe's top-grade geniuses had been German-speaking. But now, after World War Two the centre of the West no longer lay in Western Europe, but was largely displaced to the United States—where the same pattern of rapidly-accelerating growth in science, technology, and wealth became reestablished—and has now spread especially fast in the countries of South and East Asia. In the 1960s, when the history and philosophy of science were flourishing subjects, we used to argue that the extraordinary success of Western science and the culture it was inspiring depended upon its roots in the Christian doctrine of creation—a single, law-governed, intelligible natural order—and in Greek philosophy. But Japan, Hong Kong, Singapore, Taiwan, the People's Republic of China, Malaysia, and so on very quickly proved able to assimilate and develop Western technology *without* its old cultural presuppositions. They took only our science and technology: they did not need our theology or our philosophy. Nor our politics. Now we talk at world level, of *world* population, *world* economic growth, and *world* products. Not to mention *world* climate change. Our new secular eschatology is not limited to those parts of the world where the dead are buried lying flat on their backs, and with their feet towards the East from which Christ will return. No: today's secular eschatology is fully globalized. We are collectively racing faster and faster towards—what? *Global* catastrophe, presumably.

The secular globalization of eschatology means, be it noted, that any effective action to ward off, or at least defer, the great doom that threatens us has to be taken at global level. Hence its extreme difficulty, because the rivalries between nation-states and between different culture areas are so strong. When we most need a strong United Nations that organization is becoming steadily weaker and less able to enforce anything.

Eschatology has become secularized at global level, then; but it has also become personalized. A trace of *collective* belief in life after death and the supernatural world survives on the occasions when a state funeral is held, and a socially important individual is formally admitted to the national pantheon.

Interestingly, there is a certain return of traditional belief here too, in that husband and wife are permanently separated by death. In Christianity, marriage ended at death, and the couple went to Judgement separately; and similarly nowadays, the admission of one of them to the social pantheon separated the partners, so that Clementine Churchill and Denis Thatcher are soon forgotten, and people do not remember where their graves are.

What of *individual* life after death? Individual eschatology lingers chiefly in the form of a greatly enhanced awareness of transience. I am soon to die, and death is final and simple cessation. I may possibly know one day very soon that I am dying, but I'll never know that I am dead. I can be aware that I am getting close to that invisible frontier, but I'll never be aware of actually crossing it. But I am acutely aware, already, that I am doing many things for the last time, and that I shall never again walk easily, or be able to think and concentrate intensely and with a clear head. I know all the time that I am going downhill towards the invisible cliff-edge. So I know that I must love life and savour its poignant transience to the full, as I now savour the sight of the first Brimstone butterfly that I see each spring. It appears in early spring: but its emergence from hibernation is variable. A peculiarly poignant thing about the Brimstone is that *all* its beauty has never been seen, because it never sits alive with its wings spread open. Yet I have loved it all my life: because of its colour it was the original *butter*fly.

In art, I find this super-acute awareness of our transitoriness is already very common in seventeenth-century English poetry. Lives, and especially the lives of Cavalier poets, were short in those days. But I find a kindred spirit most surely when I turn to Keats, to Schubert, and to Kierkegaard. Time is short, and I must try to make something of what little I may have left, while I can: that is a modern return of the old eschatological urgency. Life itself demands that I live it to the full. While I still can.

What of the self? With the end of dogmatic metaphysics has come the end of belief in a substantial core-self, one's immortal rational soul; and this leaves a hole at the centre of the self. Since babyhood all that has ever been just *given* is the disorderly stream of raw experience. Within the buzzing, blooming confusion there are scraps of regularity and of beauty, but despite our over-optimistic talk about "self-awareness", the subject of experience is never itself actually seen. The Buddha and David Hume both understood very well the emptiness of the self. The self is not a substance; it is only a transient pattern.[23]

What is to happen to this emptiness? It can be filled with feelings, mixed feelings, and therefore feelings very often charged with ressentiment. I do not advise that, because these mixed feelings leave both the world and the self painfully at odds with themselves. Instead, I urge that the empty space of the self be filled with love, and I do *not* mean love for any finite object. I mean the love of life, the love of all experience, world-love and (best of all) love for "it all".

"It all" is perhaps the most beautiful of our English-language totalizing phrases, and the one with the richest 'idiomatic'. If you doubt me, pause and start writing down the it-all idioms. By the time you have got your first twenty idioms you will have begun to see how wide-ranging and rich they are. My own first and rather primitive list of 1999[24] contains around thirty, falling into three main groups: It all may be rich and enjoyable, as when "I love it all"; or puzzling, as when I wonder about "the meaning of it all". It may be intimidating, as when I find, "it's all a bit too much for me". But you should be able to do better than that by now. For the present I am suggesting simply that if we wish to be happy, even in the last days of humanity, and even in our own last days, we should fill the hole at the centre of the self with love for it all. It's the basis of what I have long described as "solar ethics", or ethical emotivism and expressivism. It is a determinedly non-objective and extravertive approach to ethics. Of course it is. It was taught by the early Jesus of Nazareth in the tradition of his teaching as it stood up to about the year 50, after which he who had been a critic of law-ethics was himself increasingly made into an authoritative teacher of "the law of Christ" (Galatians 6:2).[25] In the end, at Bologna from the eleventh century, the canonists took over, and as happened also in Judaism and Islam, official religious thought and action became dominated by lawyers and legalistic thinking. Christianity ended up being more or less the opposite of what Jesus had taught and lived and died for, and he remains a largely-unknown figure today. Disaster.

In our present teaching, we find that solar living and solar loving are the best "filling" for the empty self and the best relief for our anxieties about our individual and our communal destiny.

# 10
# Beliefs and Identities

During the past two centuries there has been not only huge cultural production and population growth, but also very considerable movement of peoples all around the globe. The outcome of all this today is that nearly all of us live in countries within which there is an extraordinary jumble of languages, religious sects, dating systems, narratives, organizations, values, and identities. Most people owe some allegiance to several of them, and despite their obvious contradictions are most reluctant wholly to abandon any of them. The result is that all of our allegiances have become somewhat ironical and self-mocking—whilst also being at the same time strong and sincere. If one of your allegiances overrides all the others, it is nowadays often described as your "identity"; but for other people your identity is given by your distinctive personal *mix* of allegiances.

Cambridge's first ultra-large and undenominational mega-church is currently being built, rather close to the proposed location of Cambridge's first big purpose-built mosque, and two miles south of the Cambridge United Football Club ground. After some recent success, football fans tell me with pride that Cambridge is no longer a mere university city: it is now something much grander, a real *football* city, where thousands congregate, sing hymns together, and watch a ritual being played out upon the sacred turf of the Abbey Stadium. Football, of course, is big—more than a religion, some say.

Belief is becoming strangely plural and jumbled. Many years ago the Irish intellectual Conor Cruise O'Brien was asked what the Irish really believe about life after death. He replied—oversimplifying, I think—that the Irish believe three very different things all at once: they believe that when you die you are just dead, like an animal; that when you die you become a pre-Christian, pagan ghost living in the underworld but occasionally coming up to what ordinary language might call its "old haunts"; and yet at the same time they also believe in the whole Catholic Christian eschatology. This was half-a-century ago, when the situation was relatively clear-cut. Today it is seriously muddled, and getting more so.

Even when close to being completely elbowed out, an old faith may still matter greatly to the (un)believer. John Betjeman, the popular poet, saw Christianity as consisting in the factual conviction "That God was man in Palestine / And lives today in bread and wine". In his later years he would say that he thought that this was actually *true* for no more than about half an hour in every six months. Otherwise he knew, as every moderately-educated person has known since about 1850, that it isn't all "literally true", in the strong realistic sense. Of course it isn't. It belonged to a now-lost world view. Ask yourself, who was the last person *other than Jesus* to "ascend into heaven"? I think the correct answer is that some idiot *did* paint an apotheosis of Nelson, but there has not been anyone else since. So Betjeman clung to the last shred of a faith that we all know is lost, and it *mattered* greatly to him—so much that he was always regarded as a Christian, and was buried with some ceremony at St Enodoc in Cornwall. Which is what he wanted, sort of.

It seems that what is happening is that religious beliefs, which in pre-critical days were held to be just straightforwardly true, are increasingly becoming passwords that function to protect a now-threatened but still-cherished religious identity. Every religious leader, whether he be titled an Archbishop, a Chief Rabbi, a Grand Imam, or a Lama knows that he must defend the integrity of the whole system of passwords, the "orthodoxy", for which he stands. The faithful, being nowadays severely threatened by faithlessness, look to him to be a kind of beacon, a lighthouse, a stronghold and touchstone of identity by which they can orient themselves. In short, the more senior you are as a religious leader, the more untrue to yourself you are obliged to be—and of course you know it, know it all too well. You know that you have been compelled to sacrifice your own soul or integrity, in order to help other people to (sort of) maintain theirs.

I need hardly say that I can't bear it; I cannot bear to have my head full of such an intolerable jumble of fictions, half-beliefs, and conflicting values; and the muddle is particularly debilitating in the area of eschatology because it leaves us so uncertain, unable to act decisively, and resolving instead to do little and just wait to see what happens. We are paralysed by irony.

Kierkegaard was conscious that modern people find it hard or even impossible to take any eschatological warning seriously. He pictures an enjoyable evening's entertainment at the theatre, during which a clown comes on the stage and warns the audience: a fire has broken out backstage, and they must leave the theatre at once. The audience laugh uproariously. The clown repeats his warning with tears in his eyes. The audience laughs still louder.

The interesting point about Kierkegaard's parable is that it is of course *secular*. After Kant the old Western kind of two-worlds dualism that had come down to us from Plato and the Bible was clearly coming to an end. It had to be secularized: the higher world above had to be brought down into this world. It had to be resolved into its material "basis". This was done, in rather different ways, by Hegel's Absolute Idealism, by Karl Marx, and others. Eschatology was transformed into various sorts of belief in a progressive historical liberation of humankind, or revolutionary *action* to overthrow the existing social order and free those who lived in bondage.

Notoriously, these secularized versions of the ancient Judaeo-Christian eschatology have proved to be almost as objectionable as the older supernatural beliefs. The Enlightenment and Hegelian belief in progress—the conquest of nature, the perfectibility of man and the rest—led to expansionist nationalism, imperialism and eventually to the world wars and our present environmental crisis. The Marxist version led only to the dictatorship of the proletariat, tyranny, and stagnation, and now it is dead.

In short, the problems of the old supernaturalist Great Story were not solved by secularizing Divine Providence into history. They have merely returned in new forms. So hellfire returns as global warming: but the warning is still hard to take seriously.

Can we then learn to live without any sort of historical messianism, without eschatology, and without the belief in historical progress? Can we attempt to get along by purging ourselves of the old muddle of "creeds outworn", and instead deal with our problems *ambulando*, by piecemeal small reforms and adjustments, as we become clearer about what can usefully be done?

Yes. A modest Anglo-Saxon empiricist and piecemeal approach to our cultural and environmental problems may be our best hope. But in order to see our situation clearly, and in order to help us to bear the truth and to act defectively, we need a new kind of religion. It would not be a *belief* religion, which tells us authoritatively about a better world above or in the future. It will rather be a "solar presentist" religion of wholehearted commitment to this life and to this world now. We try to live the kind of life that the early Jesus associated with "the Kingdom of God", ardent and without any ulteriority. It discards what Matthew Arnold called religion's "Hebrew old clothes", and starts instead with a full and sustained suspension of all dogmatic and ideological conviction. It starts with nihilism and art. It starts with a whole-hearted expressivist commitment to "living by the heart", to ordinary everyday humanity, and to the minimal requirements of a decent human society. It resolves that "love is the fulfilment of the law", and that we would prefer to die rather than fail in our attempt to live without ressentiment and for love only.

Thus martyrdom returns in a new form. Suppose that runaway global warming leads to a four degrees Celsius (7.2 degrees Fahrenheit) rise in temperature. On present forecasts of future fossil fuel demand we could reach this within the present century, and it could make much of the east coast of the United States and most of Africa and the Middle East uninhabitable. Suppose that the English Channel becomes crowded with boatloads of desperate refugees, migrating northwards. Will we strictly limit the numbers we admit by using force; or will we welcome and try to feed as many as we can? Many people, and many politicians, will admit that the public demand for the use of force will be irresistible. But I have suggested that we should prefer to die for our humanitarian values, rather than betray them. So martyrdom returns, because we must be as serious about humanitarian values as we used to be about our old supernatural beliefs. And I would say the same in reply to a question currently being asked in the countries bordering the north shores of the Mediterranean Sea: should we be willing to start a civil war rather than permit our own country to become Islamic and so lose all its humanitarian and Enlightenment culture and values? I still say no violence. We should prefer to risk death by arguing non-violently for a full acceptance by Islam of democratic values, critical thinking, and humanitarian ethics.

I found that last sentence hard to write: perhaps I should add that the Arab world needs a new Kemal Atatürk. We may also add that we could assist Muslims to rediscover their own religion by applying to the Holy Qur'an the same methods of lower and higher criticism and of study, that have long been applied to their own source-documents by many Western Christian scholars. In the case of Hinduism, it is well known that it was Western scholarship that first taught Gandhi to respect his own country's religious traditions. Similarly, Western scholars should publish fully critical studies of the origins and the developing theology of the Qur'an and of the *hadith*, the aim being to persuade Muslims by rational argument that a fully critical and non-realistic understanding of their own religion is much more illuminating and fruitful than the debilitating fundamentalism and backwardness of their recent history. Thus the West could revive Islam, and give Muslims their own religion; and it could be done entirely peacefully and to everyone's benefit—many Muslims themselves being already well aware of the extent to which they are trapped in relative ignorance and relative poverty by an excessively reactionary interpretation of their own religion.

After which, how are we to tidy up the disorderly remains of many different systems of eschatological belief that are still current in the modern West?

From around CE 1700 to 1900, Utopian writings, political visionaries, and scientific forecasts were mostly very optimistic about humanity's long-term future. But during the First World War the outlook began to darken. Today it is common knowledge that science fiction books and films have become very pessimistic, usually seeing a future in which our life will be dominated and perhaps severely threatened by our own technologies. Since the Second World War there have been at least fifteen scientific warnings that we are dangerously polluting our environment and need to mend our ways. The consensus is that we'll be lucky to survive what is coming over us.

It is true that in some of these cases we have heeded the warnings and have largely solved the problem, by limiting the discharge into the environment of various things from radioactivity to nitrates, insecticides, and lead. But many worries remain that have to do with over-population, leading to gradual desertification of the land and severe local fresh water shortages, and in rivers and seas to overfishing and even the extinction of many species. Over half of all the coral reefs are already gone. And there is also the question of global warming, about which Margaret Thatcher—herself a trained chemist—warned the country in a speech in 1989. Today most political and religious leaders, including the United States president and the Pope, readily acknowledge that the science is overwhelming: global warming is happening, but there is still much resistance to taking any serious action to stop it. This, together with various international rivalries and economic pressures, means that we are *collectively* much more likely than not to be presently doing much too little, much too late.

The outlook for the human future is not good. Word has gone round, and we see already many symptoms of political and economic instability. Natural disasters, the breakdown of the state, economic collapse, hunger, mass migration, and terrorism have already become everyday news.

Against this background, what of the major hopes and fears of the old religious eschatologies? There are still today a number of nations that in the past have had a messianic conception of themselves, their place in the whole human scheme of things, and their destiny. In these countries, the old religion was not very much concerned with the destiny of the individual. People's chief hope was not for their own personal immortality, but for the restoration or future establishment of the nation as a whole.

On this subject, I will say no more than that we should give up messianic nationalism. It is the very last thing humanity needs just now.

What about individual immortality, the popular hope that I, as the individual I am, will somehow survive death, and perhaps be reunited with my lost loved ones?

This concern for personal immortality was strong and remained strong between about 1850 and 1960, the most obvious symptoms of it being the vogue for spiritualism, "psychical research", and attempts to communicate with the dead. As late as the mid-twentieth century, some theologians were still arguing for personal immortality. John Baillie, a Scot, argued that if God is all-wise, all-good and all-powerful, and if each human individual is uniquely valuable and precious, then God may be expected to preserve individuals. John Hick, another Presbyterian, argued that in a world that agonized over the question of unrequited evil, the hope of a blessed life after death was the ordinary person's theodicy (or justification of the ways of God).[26] Hick, like several other theologians known to me, had suffered the worst thing of all, the loss of a child.

Today, belief that we have a metaphysical core-self, technically "a finite spiritual substance" within us, has largely been forgotten, and it seems that we all know that we are just animals and natural products of biological evolution. The detailed story of our own evolution is being filled in at a great rate. As I have indicated earlier, we are better off doing without a core-self and sticking to biology; and if we are concerned about the absence of a *metaphysical* subject within the self, then the best way to fill that internal absence is simply to fill it with outpouring universal love for "it all", for life, and for humanity. Love like that really does conquer death, and helps us to forget the self.

Thus it is possible to live without the traditional supernatural eschatology; but we must recognize that people do not like to see certain monstrous tyrants and criminals "getting away with it" and dying unpunished. They certainly should not say that they hope he rots in hell; but at the same time the state authorities do need to be vigilant in tracking down, exposing and punishing the sort of clever serial killer and sex-offender who sometimes succeeds in evading detection for many years.

Concluding this discussion, I maintain that we live in times when a global solar humanitarianism is the only faith to live by, and we should downplay and forget all merely local religious and national beliefs and identities. Identity always divides others into "brothers" and "infidels"; *we* who are all one, and *they* who are alien to us. But during the past fifty years, since about the time of the Earthrise photograph from the moon, we have begun to think of more and more things in global terms. (If you doubt me, try collecting and dating the first use of expressions like "the world economy".)

So we should now forget old identities and the belief systems associated with them. In particular, we should do without the old eschatologies, and limit ourselves to piecemeal reforms and adjustments to be made as we begin to see the need for them. And the one true faith? It is universal, beliefless solar humanitarianism, life at the end of the world, and I believe its first known prophet was the original Jesus of Nazareth. It would be irrational literally to idolize him, and he did not ask for it. Of *course* he didn't.

# 11
# Philosophy at the End of the World

As I write, in mid-2015, we are advised that all emission of carbon by the combustion of fossil fuels needs to cease by 2050 if we are to avoid catastrophic climate change. It is expected that world population will be stabilizing at that time, at about ten billion. Thereafter, we must struggle to achieve sustainability—meaning that growth must be limited to efficiency improvement within permanent limits to consumption. In the very long term, if we survive, those limits will have to be stricter, as we run out of certain rare elements. We are already running out of helium.

Can we hope to be near at least medium-term sustainability by 2050? It seems unlikely. In Asia, China and India are very large and developing fast. They find coal-fired power stations easy and attractive, and are still building them in great numbers. They are behaving like armies that hurry to get themselves into as strong a position as possible during the last days before an armistice comes into effect. They know they already have severe pollution in their great cities, but the dash for growth takes priority. Europe is lazy and slow nowadays, and may be just about the only region of the world that can happily set and achieve targets for itself that involve slowing down a little further. As for population statistics, the rapid increase in life expectancy has itself a big effect on numbers. We may not be happy to learn that we must have fewer and fewer babies because the world is filling up with more and more old people.

The outlook is not good, and I suggest that acute world-wide political and economic instability has already arrived and will get worse. Before science-based industrial civilization began, the old religions did offer the hope of other-worldly salvation to troubled and unhappy humans; but today those old faiths are fatally weakened. This-worldly political hopes, whether socialist, liberal, or anarchist, have also failed. No wonder working people are uneasy and discontented.

Can philosophy help? As was remarked earlier, many in the West have failed to notice that with the Death of God the Creator we have also lost the belief that we have a ready-made, law-governed, created world, shaped by him expressly to suit our needs. If there is no Creator, there is no Creation.

Philosophy itself took a long time to grasp the point here. The founder of modern philosophy, René Descartes, made the great shift from the Middle Ages to modernity by starting his philosophy not with God, but within finite, thinking individual human subjects, who construct for themselves their own knowledge of their own world.

The main difficulty arose quickly. There was never much doubt about the objectivity of *God's* knowledge of the world he had made, because the divine mind was understood to be all-encompassing and all-knowing. Humans are finite, and do not have the sort of total "inside" and immediate knowledge that was attributed to God. The physicist may build a mathematical model of the way the world works, but how does he or she check that the information the sense-organs seem to be relaying about the external world is accurate? How can we check that our interior picture of the world is an adequate representation or copy of it? We cannot jump out of our own heads to check what's really out there. We have always and only ever been *inside* our own heads, and we never have the god's eye view.

Descartes responded by proving the existence of God, and arguing that God is not a deceiver. God has given us the conviction that we are set in a world that is objectively real, and that our senses tell us about it. So we must rely upon God.

Thus Descartes invented the modern notion of "objective reality", and at the same time invoked God as the guarantor of it. In the technical vocabulary, God guaranteed epistemological *realism*, the belief in the mind-independent reality of the objects of our knowledge.

It didn't last: in philosophy a move like that of Descartes is sure to be challenged. Two philosophers, Hume and Kant, set out to test whether they could find a secular justification of the objectivity of our knowledge that would *not* require God to guarantee it. (It is pretty clear to the reader that both of them knew that the time had come for philosophy to break free from theology.) Hume was not quite successful, and ended up as a moderate sceptic who said that we must simply fall back upon our "natural belief" in realism. Kant did more, in the most spectacularly ambitious and demanding of all Western books since Aristotle, *The Critique of Pure Reason* (1781). Newton's extraordinary achievement in constructing a mathematic physics that did work and was plainly right convinced Kant that we do have objective knowledge. Therefore we are capable of it. But how? Kant set out to demonstrate, by an analysis of unsurpassed pure intellectual power, how the mind must process the chaos of experience in order to make it into objective knowledge of a real world. In short, in very short: we impose order upon our raw experience. We are the world-makers, we confer objectivity, we lay down all the rules. We have built our world, out of nothing more than the chaos you can see if for a few moments you screw up your eyes and look closely at the inside of your eyelids.

A simple analogy from computing makes the point well. The input of raw data from experience is processed by the programming in our heads, and thereby turned into an ordered world.

To work it all out, Kant used a special method of regressive or "transcendental" analysis, by repeatedly asking for the possibility-conditions, as if he believed in a standard programming that *logically* has to be the same in every human head. After him, others took up his account, and made it more historical and culturalist. They said: "It is the *cultural* programming in your head that leads you to build your world and to see everything in the way you do." By the twentieth century others were saying: "When we learn to use our native *language*, and then also other related sign-systems such as mathematics, we are being inducted into a way of life and a world-picture." The world hangs suspended within the language in which we describe it, a language which is of course always gradually evolving as our whole world-picture evolves.[27]

This last view is not realistic, but nor is it sceptical. Our world-picture starts with what's in ordinary language, but over the centuries it has been greatly elaborated by science and enriched by artists. It is not arbitrary. It has been developed over millennia, and it works. It has always worked. And it is, as they say, *quite good enough to be going on with*. We can give it our provisional trust, but it is only *our* world. It is not *the* world, absolutely. Our knowledge is always fallible, and open to review and correction.

Curiously, the fact that "the real world" is now so transient and man-made makes it only the more poignantly beautiful.

Such is the human condition. Collectively, we are the builders of our world; and it is obvious to all that the worlds that people build together also reflect their religious beliefs. When you are in Saudi Arabia, you are in a major part of the Muslim world. The world of Irish and Italian peoples is Catholic, the world of Scandinavia and the United States is historically Protestant, India is Hindu, and so on—and you will note that we tend nowadays to appraise a religion by looking at the kind of human social world it typically creates.

Since about the year 1800 CE the picture has been complicated by the rise of science-based, machine-powered industrial society, and by a storm of very rapid cultural change. More than ever, we learn to see our world as a large-scale reflection of ourselves, and we have been uneasy since the early and mid-nineteenth century about the sheer accelerating pace of cultural change and "de-traditionalization". The fear that we may be heading for an almighty crash has been particularly strongly felt since Hiroshima.

All this explains why, in the case of the greenhouse effect/ global warming/climate change, we notice a certain return of the language of religion. "If you do not quickly repent and mend your ways, you will fry", we are told. Formerly, we would fry in hell, but today we are told that we will fry on earth. That is secularization. There is excellent scientific evidence, such as no rational person who takes the trouble to inform himself or herself can dismiss, that the threat of climate change is real and urgent. Broadly speaking, governments accept it and even try to act upon it. But the threat, interestingly, reaches us clothed in echoes of religious language and feeling.

A curious sign of this return of ancient religious ideas is that the threat remains perpetually about equally urgent. Time was already short, and we should *hurry*, when I was first told about the greenhouse effect in the 1970s, the question was urgent when Mrs Thatcher first devoted a speech to it in 1989, and time is still short today. This is what a New Testament scholar might call "eschatological urgency". Its modern return reveals the extent to which we highly-secularized modern Westerners are still influenced by ancient religious patterns of thinking.

Our technology has been too greedy, too ruthlessly exploitative, and in too much of a hurry. We will probably do too little, too late to avert the crash that looms ahead of us. It will be a Judgement upon us, and the whole human race is likely to find itself struggling to get through a very painful period. Gradually, we will have to develop the energy to build a new and better world. It will have to be astonishingly different from our present world, its most conspicuous feature being that it will not be so dominated by the love of power as our present, doomed world has been.

# 12

# Our Fall into Environmental Crisis—and Our Redemption

Since the atomic bombs were dropped on Hiroshima and Nagasaki in 1945, a dark cloud has hovered over the future of humanity. Briefly, it is the fear that we human beings have come too far, too fast in the last two or three centuries, and are now in danger of being destroyed by our own technologies. We have already partly ruined our planet, and are so preoccupied with our competition with each other that we prefer not to think about the rate at which we are stripping the land and the sea of their resources.

The threat of a looming catastrophe is, then, our new eschatology, and it is a judgement that we are evidently bringing upon ourselves. But it is multi-facetted, and at any one time most of the public's attention is apt to be focussed upon just one of its facets. At present, that facet is the greenhouse effect/global warming/climate change, about which there is still quite a storm of controversy. The majority of governments around the world are sufficiently persuaded that there is real cause for concern here to be prepared to make at least some moves towards decarbonizing the economy; but several other environmental issues which are not quite so salient just at present have not gone away, and may at any time return and give us a nasty jolt. For example, the final disappearance of the great apes who are our nearest kin will be a cultural disaster. A solar flare that knocked out our communications satellites would cause very great disruption. Low-level chemical pollution of fresh water by our medications could one day have a serious effect upon our fertility. Desertification of once-fertile land by overgrazing and soil exhaustion still continues. There are few sadder and more horrible sights than the spectacle of magnificent sharks being caught, having their big pectoral fins hacked off to make soup, and then being thrown back dying into the sea.

Enough: that is part of the reason why our discussion so far has been so diffuse and multi-stranded. We are touching upon so many sensitive issues. I saw, in about 1950, in a sea lough in County Cork in Ireland, that the ordinary rocky coastlines in the western parts of the British Isles were once at least as rich in exotic life as any coral reef. I saw it, and it was so astonishing that I seem to see it still. From the same period, I remember what the flying insect life of England was—perhaps especially in the flower meadows of the chalk downland before they were ploughed up. From glowworms to slowworms, the creatures I loved are no longer part of the experience of childhood, and their names are now being cut out of children's dictionaries to make way for the technical terms of the digital future.

Those creatures will not return. But in speaking of a diffuse and many-stranded discussion I was doing more than just expressing nostalgia for a richer but now lost pre-industrial world. I was referring to the way Darwin, Malthus and others succeeded in "keeping many balls in the air at once" as they worked out their big organizing theories of how the world works. The unifying idea we have in mind for our present topic is sustainability, a way of life that does not exploit and exhaust the resources of the environment, but that remains in long-term balance with nature. Already we are making the necessary transition here, as we learn habitually to recycle, restock, and replant everything we have taken from nature. This immediately calls to mind the old transition in Western thought from history (which moves on, because it is disciplinary, future-oriented, linear, and progressive) to "the Kingdom of God" or post-history (which is no longer teleological because it doesn't seek a future consummation, but instead rests in a consummation at which it has already arrived). Our tradition always envisaged rest after strife and stability after the end of our journeying. So we are talking about a realized eschatology, which experiences "the Last Things" as being already present.

This stable historical period is in my own terminology "anthropomonist". It is an age of "empty radical humanism", because there is no longer a strong ethical self, a will to power that strives to attain a future goal. Instead there is an empty self, its empty centre being filled simply with love for "it all". This kind of self will be capable of solar living, the ethic of those who are already at life's destination, and are content with self-expression and communion with others. We are not battling to increase our own dominance: we have become content with art and love.

My aim in introducing these religious and philosophical strands into the discussion has been to suggest that when we talk of climate change we are not speaking only of a straightforward large-scale scientific *prediction*, like the prediction of an eclipse or the reappearance of a comet. No, because global warming is a prediction made in the human world, and it refers to present human behaviour and future human experiences. As soon as the prediction has been made, it begins to affect people's thinking and planning, and we see that it needs to be understood as being conditional: "If we go on as we are doing, we risk bringing disaster upon ourselves and upon the planet." It is therefore not simply a *prediction*, but a conditional forecast and a moral admonition intended to make us think: "We can't go on like this. We need to change ourselves, and the way we act upon our world." Thus what began as a rather simple extrapolation turns into a very big ethical and religious demand.

A further, but difficult bit of philosophy: in the generations since Darwin's *Origin of Species* was published we have gradually come to see ourselves as completely interwoven with and part of the world of nature. The biblical picture of nature as a *plenum*, a complete ready-made divine creation, into which we have been inserted (with adult minds already educated into linguistic fluency, and even already capable of philosophical knowledge of God!) had to be dropped. Instead, we see ourselves as having emerged gradually within nature, which was at first only a turbid stream of lived preconscious and prelinguistic experience, within which as we learnt to talk we gradually differentiated our world away from ourselves, and ourselves away from our world. We did it all from within, and without any guidance at all—and to this day there remains a sense in which we and our world always mirror each other. *And we made both.* If things are going very badly wrong with our world, that's because our world is a projected-out image of ourselves. Here is a new it-all idiom: "It is all our fault." Thus we need—in an excellent popular phrase already quoted—to "change our whole attitude to life", if we are to put our world to rights and to ensure for ourselves a long-term future. That means a *religious conversion*.

Most discussion of global warming today is mathematical, in accordance with the pattern laid down by Galileo, Descartes, and Newton. Science is natural philosophy, and its method applies mathematical principles to the natural phenomena. From observations and the mathematical laws of nature we deduce predictions—and that's that. To the standard scientific account I am adding only the comment that when we start predicting future events in the human world, events in which we are ourselves going to be involved, then the published prediction itself becomes a causal factor in the situation. One utters the prediction not to say to us: "Do nothing, and the prediction will be fulfilled, and you'll see that I am right", but to say: "Unless you do something urgently, you, and indeed all of us, will suffer the consequences that the prediction describes." The predictor is not just a scientific forecast, but is uttering an admonition, a prophetic warning. Good scientific backing can be claimed for the warning, but the purpose is not chiefly an interest in testing the theory against experience; it is an interest in getting us to change our behaviour. And the prophet is probably very well aware that the moral change called for here is very big indeed, because we are so passionately attached to our powered transport, our artificial lighting and heating, our recorded sound and moving pictures, and all the rest. The modern energy industries are huge, and not easily budged. The lead time for any substantial change is several decades long. Thus the issues at stake here are at once so large-scale that they involve the oil majors, hundreds of billions of dollars, and big international conferences, but they are also so intimate and searching that they require of us a *religious* response. Are we ready to change our desires and our habits of living?

Global warming is a world economic and political issue, and it is also a *religious* issue, in which we see a certain return of traditional theological patterns of thinking. As when, for example, we find that we must call for repentance, *metanoia*, if we are to persuade people that they really must change *themselves*, if we are all of us to change the world before it's too late.

Are we ready to consider trying to change ourselves on the scale required? No: on the whole we are not. Politically, the Greens are always a minority party. Our attachment to a high-consumption way of life is so strong that it resembles an addiction. People en masse are not going to be able to give it all up, just like that. Instead, as happens also with clean air, with obesity, and with drink and tobacco, it will be for governments to use an array of public health measures, sticks and carrots, and the like, gradually to nudge us all in the direction of a sustainable collective lifestyle for the future. Writers and artists can contribute encouraging pictures to help us all along.

So that's all right, isn't it? No, not quite, because, as we have feared all along, it seems that we do and always will do too little too late. Token efforts are made to conserve the big game animals of Africa and Asia, the apes, the big cats and bears, and the whales; but is it not everywhere the case that we suspect that the battles will in the end be lost? Consider what has happened already to the Galapagos Islands. It is now too late, much too late, to conserve the islands as Darwin found them. And the same is true of almost all aspects of environmental concern. Ordinary people are not going to be converted to environmentalism on the necessary scale, and governments can and will do something but they cannot and will not do enough. In particular, the governments of the biggest countries will not do enough.

The next possibility to be considered is that we might look to militant environmental activists, the Jesuits, or shock troops of environmentalism, to give a lead. In many large international organisations such as Greenpeace and the Friends of the Earth people have been trying to do this for years, and have at least succeeded in winning a good deal of public sympathy. But they have not in fact stopped the Japanese and Norwegian whalers, and after some decades one may perhaps suggest that these organisations have peaked and are now in decline. They too have slowly lost their wars of attrition.

Yet another possibility: about fifteen centuries ago, in both Greek and Latin Christianity, and in Buddhism all around the Himalayan region, religious orders sought out and built their monasteries in places as remote and inaccessible as possible. These were places in which religious and civil values might be preserved in hard times. Offshore islands and steep mountainsides were favoured, and in a few cases the communities still survive. Might it be possible today for our surviving world religions to do something similar? The communities might look a little like Israeli *kibbutzim,* and might be established in some quiet northern corners of Canada or Greenland that are just becoming fit for farming. If they can survive the coming catastrophe, they may be able to lead the remnants of the human race out of it once again, as they did before.

To which one may reply with one word: Lampedusa, Italy's island near the Libyan coast, which nowadays is daily crowded with thousands of refugees and asylum-seekers struggling to get into Europe. The coming disaster will be world-wide, and the millions of desperate refugees will be flooding everywhere as they look for some place where they can still hope to live. Very soon there will be no places left to hide. Even the super-rich will not be safe.

It is true, however, that many religious leaders today do recognise that the wide-ranging issues that we cluster together under the headings of "global warming" and the "environmental crisis" are issues that do present humankind with a *religious* challenge. They would genuinely like to do something if they could see clearly what it is to be. In reply, it seems that there are three main lines of attack. In all faith communities people can work out eco- or green theologies that may stir the popular imagination and encourage people to become more active. Politicians can be lobbied and persuaded to use more public health-type measures that will slowly change popular habits. And there need to be experiments with small communities trying out and developing new green lifestyles.

Might all this help? It will probably be tried. Indeed, many people will say that they are already doing all these things. But alas, it will not be enough.

Our emerging condition is beginning to recall that in which Christian finds himself at the beginning of *The Pilgrim's Progress*.[28] He reads a book, and trembles. He goes home to his wife and children, and says to them: "I am for certain informed that this our City will be burned with fire from Heaven, in which fearful overthrow (all of us) shall miserably come to ruin ... except some way of escape can be found." Christian continues in his distressed state for some days, and his relatives fear for his sanity. But then he meets a man named Evangelist, who tells him that he must "fly from the wrath to come". Evangelist points out the way he must take, and a narrow gate through which he must pass in order to find salvation. Christian begins to run in that direction. He will not pause to listen to those who try to call him back, but runs on, crying, "Life, Life, Eternal Life!"

If, as seems quite probable, a time comes, in half a century or so, when our own plight begins to look very like the plight of Christian in *The Pilgrim's Progress*, then it may well be that religious conservatives will seek to exploit the similarity. They will argue that runaway global warming is a Divine Judgement upon us for our many sins. But they will be wrong, because the two cases are profoundly different. Christian fled away from the doomed City of Destruction, set upon a plain like the cities of the biblical plain, Sodom and Gomorrah. Our situation is quite different, because we have ourselves created the whole disastrous situation, "it all". We cannot fly away from ourselves, and there is no refuge outside ourselves. The arrival of this ultimate realised eschatology finds humanity radically alone at the end of the world. We mis-made ourselves, and we are bringing disaster upon ourselves. Who can usefully blame whom, and what can be done?

The situation is alarming, and the revelation of extreme human solitude, greatness, and littleness in the last days of humanity is very challenging. I have hinted at the parallel cases, in biblical theology, of Adam as he stands convicted of sin and sentenced to expulsion from Eden, and of Jesus as he is sentenced to die horribly for his teaching, alone and undelivered from his fate. Our own prospect is, if anything, even worse than that of Adam and that of the Second Adam, Jesus. In us the human being reaches the summit of self-knowledge and solitary dignity, in a moment, which is also to be our utter ruin. At the end of the world, Man stands forth alone, to be chopped down. Peak and crash coincide. It is a cosmic tragedy.

At such a moment, which may come in about a century from now (or rather less), is there anything at all left for us humans to affirm, to cling to, and to do? To the end, we must continue with our solar affirmation of life, and our attempt to practise a solar humanitarian ethic of unconditional love. That's the only hope there is, and the only hope that there can possibly be. The individual human must hope that he or she can go out on a top note, and as members of the collective *Humanum* we cannot hope to do better than that. Die with a bang! That's the best *martyria*.[29]

But in the end we human beings messed up. We started well, when in the primal chaos the first motion of the first signs began to shed the first flickers of light. Gradually, as signs and their motions multiplied, we began to emerge, as we laboriously differentiated ourselves on the near side of language from our emergent world on the far side. Gradually we became aware of the earth's beauty, of the joys of life, and of human love. But we always had to fight for a living; hunger, disease, and extreme violence were seldom far away. Slowly we stabilised and enriched our life with religion, art, and cultural pride. When we invented science we began to believe that it might be possible to use our new technologies to give most people a better life. But that dream has been only partially successful, and in only some and not all parts of our world. Now we see that we rushed modernity, and did not give ourselves enough time. We were in too much of a hurry. Now, it is apparently all coming to an end. Well, we always knew that we were only transients. Perhaps we can disappear collectively, and also individually, saying that on the whole we have loved life, and are grateful to life, for life.[30]

And there is one lesson we have learnt from these reflections. Although our modern secular eschatology is different from the popular eschatology of his own period, the ethical teaching of the original Jesus, short of its supernatural dress, and now recently reconstructed, is even more interesting and relevant to our day than it was to people in his own day. Perhaps he may get a better hearing now than he got then. He's waited a long time for it.

# Notes and Further Reading

Although when young I did specialize in the study of Natural Science for five years, this book is not about the *science* of global warming. Rather, it has been prompted by the general public's lack of interest in the whole subject, and the complete absence of any very serious ethical and religious response to what may be a very dark prospect facing us all. So far as the general factual background is concerned, two good and reliable guides are Al Gore, who produced the documentary film project, *An Inconvenient Truth* (2006), and the writings of the very-industrious and sober Nicholas Stern, author of *The Economics of Climate Change* (Cambridge: The Cambridge University Press, 2007) and the more popular *A Blueprint for a Safer Planet* (London: The Bodley Head, 2009; Vintage Books/Random House ed., 2010). Stern represents the very highest level of advice given to politicians.

Martin Rees, *Our Final Century* (London: Heinemann, 2003) is a good summary by a senior scientist. In Britain the best-known global-warming sceptic is Nigel Lawson, *An Appeal to Reason: A Cool Look at Global Warming* (London: Duckworth, 2008). Naomi Klein, *This Changes Everything* (London: Allen Lane, 2014) is big and thorough, but it blames 'capitalism'. There is I think no book which, like this one, is interested in the way in which our current debates echo ancient religious anxieties about "the end of the world", or which asks why most people seem unable to treat the topic with sustained seriousness. (After assenting to the main line of argument most people go back to their cars and to their hopes and plans for future economic growth, and entirely forget about the subject.) I try also to connect the whole topic with our traditional anxieties about the contingency and transience of everything, looking for an appropriately existential response, and wondering what form an eschatology for today should take. How, for example, can we be world-affirming and ethically active in the face of very large-scale disaster?

Here my notes are not intended to be bookish or academic, but only to indicate just a few interesting sidelines of thought.

1. I refer in particular to Russell Hoban's *Ridley Walker*, Doris Lessing's *Memoirs of a Survivor*, and Cormac MacCarthy's *The Road*. These are the three novels that came first to mind, and there are many others.

2. The Belgian painter René Magritte says: "There is a mystery in our life—but *what is it?*" The mystery is so deep that we don't know what it is, or how to describe it.

3. Not present, in the sense of here and now, but *to present*, the verb: put on a show, come out.

4. For example, with the Stoics.

5. Peacock may have been one of the first to suggest that we might be destroyed by industrial pollution.

6. Friedrich Nietzsche, *The Will to Power*, Walter Kaufmann ed. (New York: Vintage Books/Random House, 1967), p.7.

7. In the chapter titled "The Grand Inquisitor".

8. See my *Jesus and Philosophy* (London: SCM Press, 2009).

9. Notice in cinema how the threat of our technology to us is personified in the figure of a fearsome and hugely powerful man-machine, a "terminator".

10. I have been developing this radically new interpretation of Jesus and of Christianity for a decade now, but it is so strange to most people that I have been unable as yet to get it noticed and discussed. I hope that in another generation or so there may be people who can understand it.

11. From his period as a student with Russell, Wittgenstein retained a very strong conviction that it is impossible strictly to prove the truth of negative factual statements. Therefore on a famous occasion he obstinately refused to admit that there was *not* an elephant in the room. In which case the everyday use of the phrase "the elephant in the room" is badly garbled.

12. The interesting thought that the traditional God of the Philosophers is himself a philosophical idealist, because God's own Mind encompasses everything and has no outside, never quite occurred to orthodox theists, and still does not occur to them. Hegel, of course, must have recognized the point.

13. Newton's title—which shows us what *he* meant by science. The leading physicists today remain mathematicians rather than experimentalists, but by building the LHC (Large Hadron Collider) at CERN they are showing their continuing desire to perform experiments if they can get the necessary funds to do so.

14. The closing lines of *In Memoriam A. H. H.*, showing that Tennyson's own eschatological beliefs had become reduced and vague. He still clung to what little was left to him.

15. In his most recent big book Pinker argues that over the centuries human beings have become a little less violent and more kind to each other. He's right. I agree.

16. Nicholas Stern's *Blueprint,* pp. 16–19, gives a brief summary of the way in which, during the nineteenth century, the role of carbon dioxide, water vapour, and other gases in creating a "greenhouse effect" came to be understood.

17. I am told that the reason why Professor McKenzie's name is unknown to the general public is that he cares only for science, and has never sought popular fame.

18. Some late-Victorian English churchmen considered the possibility of religious communities composed of married couples: "the religious life" but without *celibacy.* I am adding the idea of the religious life—perhaps especially for women—without *children,* and thinking of several notable artists of the twentieth century. I have in mind the examples of two important sculptors and one great painter.

19. Etymologically, a "world" is the age of a man, the milieu in which he lives. The use of "world" as synonymous with (sometimes) "the planet", or "the cosmos", is secondary. I sometimes picture our world as being made to seem real by having our descriptive and evaluative language plastered all over it. Imagine a papier maché model, made of old letters, newspapers, books and advertisements. Once again, the chaos of experience plus the to and fro of language equals our world.

20. Herbert Butterfield, *Christianity and History* (London: Methuen, 1948).

21. If the bodily resurrection of Jesus from his grave had really happened, and there really were a large group of thoroughly reliable witnesses, it would surely have been a major, major historical event. Er, wouldn't it? Nobody in Classics seems to think so. Perhaps since the sixteenth century we have all been tacit non-realists about the Resurrection of Jesus. I suspect that the resurrection stories are not really about Jesus at all. They are about who is top cleric, and they broadly answer: Peter. He was first.

22. In about 1941, Von Ribbentrop is said to have put out feelers about a move away from the regime's Foreign Ministry,

because he feared that soon the whole world would be German and he would be out of a job: an extraordinary bit of *folie de grandeur*.

23. Gilbert Ryle, in *The Concept of Mind* (London: Methuen, 1949), speaks of "the systematic elusiveness of the 'I'". There is no mirror inside my skull that my soul can look into in order to see itself and find out what it looks like.

24. In *The Meaning of It All in Everyday Speech* (London: SCM Press, 1999). Go through the list of the idioms at the end of the book.

25. A bit unfair to St Paul, who himself says enough to have justified the permanent exclusion from the Christian tradition of the idea of religious law. Love is the fulfilling of the law, is it not?

26. John Baillie, brother of another Scottish theologian, Donald Baillie, was the author of *And the Life Everlasting*. John Hick, who became internationally very well known, tried to answer the question of verification by replying that our faith will be finally and decisively verified after death, and not before. Thus personal immortality was an idea necessary to his thought throughout his long career. For his developed belief about it see Hick's *Death and Eternal Life*.

27. Although the British have usually been wary of *philosophical* anti-realism, it has been common doctrine amongst the poets at least since Wordsworth. I am particularly fond of Walter de la Mare, who states it very well. Look, for example, at "Self to Self", in *Collected Poems* (London: Faber and Faber, 1942; Eleventh impression, 1954), pp. 181–82. Amongst my own, much younger, contemporaries I have noted similar ideas in Simon Armitage and Robert MacFarlane.

28. I quote from the opening pages of the edition of Bunyan's *Pilgrim's Progress and Grace Abounding*, edited for the Oxford University Press by Edmund Venables and re-edited by Mabel Peacock (1940). It keeps the original spelling and marginalia, and is well edited.

29. Alluding to *martus*, witness and *martyria*, martyrdom, in conscious opposition to the popular use of "martyrdom" today in connection with suicide bombing. In the end we made a bit of a mess of the human experiment, but there was also in it much that was truly great and wonderful. I hope we will not forget all that, and that most of us will feel able to say at the end, "I am glad to have lived, and to have been part of all that."

30. I have ended with the worst-case scenario as being now the one that seems the most probable. But there remains also the other main possibility, that by a continuing process of piecemeal adaptation we will successfully defer catastrophe and survive for long enough to attain full sustainability. My own country is notorious for somehow muddling through. In my closing paragraphs I echo Nietzsche's great test of whether he himself could and did say a wholehearted yes to his own life. Could he say yes to the Eternal Return of the same? Supposed he had to endure all his sufferings again and again, world without end? He answered yes! I am suggesting that a religious person caught up in the final days of humanity can similarly say that in spite of all humanity's wickedness, folly, and undeserved sufferings there has been enough in our world of beauty, goodness, and joy to make it all just about worthwhile. After a life of suffering, Wittgenstein sent a final message to his remaining few students: "Tell them I've had a wonderful life!"

# Index of Names
# and
# Principal Themes

Adam, the Second Adam, the Son of Man, the Last Man, the *Humanum*.
 Terms, mainly from St Paul (Romans 5) that evoke human solidarity.
 'In Adam' we are divided by language and ethnicity, but in the second
 renewed humanity we are 'all one'. I revive these biblical ideas in con-
 nection with our remaking of ourselves after climate catastrophe — chs.
 3, 4, pp. 55f., 68
Anthropocene epoch in geology, beginning AD 1610. The period in which
 human activities have become the main influence upon the Earth's geol-
 ogy — 14, 54
Apocalypse. A written account of a seer's vision of future events. In the
 New Testament 'Apocalypse' = 'Revelation'. Otherwise, see *catastrophe*
Aristotle — 41, 68
Arnold, Matthew — 85
Ataturk, K. — 86
Attlee, Clement — 20
Auden, W. H. — 8
Baillie, John B. — 88
Bartholomew I, Patriarch of Constantinople — 61
Beethoven, Ludwig van — 19, 77
Betjeman, John — 82
Blair, Tony — 42, 53
Blake, William — 31
Buddha — 79

# About the Author

**Don Cupitt** is a Life Fellow of Emmanuel College, Cambridge UK—John Harvard's college. As an undergraduate he studied successively natural sciences, theology and philosophy. He was ordained to the Anglican priesthood in 1960, but in 1962 he returned to Cambridge to teach and, since then, has stayed put. A frequent broadcaster, mainly for the BBC, he has made three TV Series, one of which, "The Sea of Faith," (1984), also gave rise to a book and to an international network of radical Christians which is still growing. He is the author of more than fifty books, including *Creative Faith* (2015), *Jesus and Philosophy* (2009), and *Above Us Only Sky* (2008).

Lightning Source UK Ltd.
Milton Keynes UK
UKHW020659280519
343440UK00003B/5/P